AN OPINIONATED GUIDE

BRITISH FAMILY ESCAPES

Alice Tate

HOXTON MINI PRESS

From the publisher:

LONG LIVE OPINION

This series of guide books is designed to give you as little information as possible. In fact, we make every effort to leave places we don't *really* love out and cut out superfluous facts. Aren't we nice? Well, it's our conviction that in a world of too much information, well-formed opinion is like a much-reduced sauce: tasty and filling. We have two young kids: we adore them, we are shattered by them. These are the places we'd visit to find some calm while exciting them. Double whammy. Just our opinion, though.

Ann and Martin, London, 2023
(Above: with their children Hazel, 3 and Olive, 5)

From the author:

BRITAIN IS MARVELLOUS

Greetings, fellow parent. You might have waved goodbye to long lie-ins and meditation retreats (plus your luggage is mainly toys now) but there's still plenty to get excited about. What makes the places in this book special is that they welcome families with open arms but won't feel like a compromise. From luxurious hotels to comfortable campsites, there's a solid mix of wallet-friendly stays and we-can-dream escapes, so whatever you're after there's something here that you (and your kids) will love.

Alice Tate, London, 2023
(Above: with her child Kit, 8 months)

THE DESTINATIONS

Opposite: Glen Dye Cabin & Cottages (no.29)
Above: Barsham Barns (no.40)

Opposite: Harwarden Estate (no.25)
Above: FForest Farm (no.26)

Opposite: Birch (no.2)
Above: Harwarden Estate (no.25)

THE BEST FOR...

SEASIDE ESCAPES
Go armed with buckets and spades to Hope Cove House (no.24), which sits above an idyllic sheltered swimming cove in Devon. Barsham Barns (no.40) is perfectly placed for exploring Norfolk's wild and sandy coast, Three Mile Beach (no.10) overlooks one of Cornwall's finest stretches, or check in to CABÜ by the Sea (no.8) for a self-catered seafront stay a stone's throw from the shingled shore of Dungeness.

CITY STAYS
Cities and families don't always go hand in hand but The Hoxton, Southwark (no.6) takes the stress out of a London adventure with its Tiny Hox offering, and the tipis at No.1 by Guesthouse (no.32) will make tiny travellers feel like royalty in York. Artist Residence (no.20) puts you right where you want to be in the hippest neighbourhood for exploring Bristol, and you're on the doorstep of Manchester's theatreland at Kimpton Clocktower (no.35).

GETTING OUTDOORS
Forage and learn bushcraft at Glen Dye Cabins & Cottages (no.29), cook by candlelight and stroll through the nature reserve at Fforest (no.26), bring the binoculars to birdwatch at Elmley Nature Reserve (no.1), and hone kids' adventurous spirit at Hawarden Estate Experience (no.25).

GROUNDS & GARDENS
The walled kitchen gardens at Middleton Lodge (no.31) and Chewton Glen (no.9) are all the inspiration green fingered little ones will need to get gardening. The Grove's (no.7) extensive grounds are so vast you'll never need to leave, and Gleneagles' (no.30) 850 acres of fields, streams and hills are home to extensive outdoor pursuits.

ON-SITE ACTIVITIES
If you like your family holidays to be action-packed, there's plenty to keep everyone busy at Birch (no.2), from pottery throwing to doughnut decorating. There's every outdoor activity you can think

of at Gleneagles (no.30), wild safari adventures at Port Lympne Hotel & Reserve (no.3), woodland treasure trails at Hawarden Estate Experience (no.25), and there's even indoor soft play at Tredethick Farm Cottages (no.22).

SWITCHING OFF
Go off-grid and enjoy a digital detox at Cynefin Retreats (no.38), where you can embrace doing not a whole lot besides soaking up the serene views. West Cawthorne Barns (no.33) is just as tranquil, with the North York Moors on the doorstep, and for a really remote retreat, Milovaig House (no.27) is somewhere to savour the wild beauty of the Isle of Skye.

LUXURY/ SPECIAL OCCASIONS
Book in for a Bamford spa treatment at The Grove (no.7), upgrade to a treehouse at Chewton Glen (no.9), and dip your toes into luxury lakeside life at Lakes by Yoo (no.16). Kids will have to clear their calendars to fit everything in at Gleneagles (no.30), while you hit the spa.

KIDS' CLUBS
Everyone deserves the chance to relax, and if that means fitting in a bit of child-free time you'll want to make the most of the toy-filled Playbarn at Calcot & Spa (no.14), 90 minutes of free childcare a day at Moonfleet Manor (no.21) and Fowey Hall (no.23), and Gleneagles' (no.30) brilliant Little Glen crèche.

OLDER KIDS
Tweens and teens aren't always the easiest holiday companions, but they'll be eager to show off their new surfing skills at Watergate Bay (no.11), join you for stand-up paddleboarding lessons at Another Place (no.34), make holiday friends at The Farm at Avebury (no.12), spend a day shadowing a safari ranger at Port Lympne (no.3), and enjoy running barefoot and feral at Fforest (no.26).

UNDER THREES
Tinies will find everything that makes their world go round at Tredethick Farm Cottages (no.22), from soft play to petting animals and a toasty indoor swimming pool. There are family frills aplenty at Fowey Hall (no.23) and Moonfleet Manor (no.21), and all the parenting paraphernalia you could possibly need for babies and toddlers at Calcot & Spa (no.14).

I

ELMLEY NATURE RESERVE

Bell tents, cottages and cabins on a tranquil nature reserve

Peace and quiet aren't words you usually associate with a family holiday, but dare we say they're on the cards here; it's a real escape from the daily grind and feels remote, even though its only 40 miles from London. Set in 3,300 acres of wilderness on an island in North Kent, Elmley is run by Gareth and Georgina Fulton, who have continued their family's 40-plus years spent restoring the landscape to allow biodiversity to flourish. Luckily for the rest of us, they've added some accommodation so we can enjoy it too. Blending seamlessly into the landscape are traditional shepherds' huts, custom-built cabins and bell tents, or you can stay in a five-bedroom cottage or the 18th-century farmhouse (for over-10s only). This is somewhere to completely switch off and connect with nature, cook outdoors, stargaze, and enjoy family walks among the wildlife.

Elmley, Minster on Sea, Sheerness ME12 3RW
elmleynaturereserve.co.uk

ROOMS   Tucked among the trees, the Woodland Bell Tents are a family favourite for their fun sense of adventure. They sleep two adults and two children and are available through the summer from May to September. They're fully powered (always useful when travelling with kids) and have floor-level beds with heavy duvets and pillows, lanterns, kettles, outdoor fire pits, Bramley products and Falcon enamelware for your morning brew. Washing facilities are communal for the bell tents, so if that's a turn off you might prefer the larger huts, with their own bathrooms, log burning stoves, standard-height beds and outdoor tubs.

FOOD   The bell tents and huts have modest self-catering facilities. Breakfast hampers can be delivered, which include fresh croissants and eggs, while lunch and snacks are available at The Cowshed Cafe from 12–3pm daily, with soups, sausage rolls, hot pots and soft drinks on offer. In the winter the Farmhouse Kitchen and Dining room is reserved for adults and children over 10 though delicious dinners can be delivered to your hut. In the summer, Kingshill Barn is open to all ages. Fresh, seasonal ingredients are used and local suppliers championed, with Kent's bounty showcased throughout the menu.

ACTIVITIES   The scenery here is beautiful, so pack your raincoats because walks (whatever the weather) are a must. Paths are easy to follow and flat, so little legs won't struggle, and there are bird hides along the way for watching a variety of feathered friends. Elmley also hosts nature-based activities for kids through the school holidays, from pond-dipping to owl spotting, and you can book a wildlife safari experience or join walks with one of Elmley's nature guides.

NEARBY   You're not too far from Faversham, which is lovely for a stroll, or Whitstable, which has no shortage of excellent places to pick up fresh seafood and vinegary chips to enjoy on the pebbly beach. There's also Leeds Castle, which is a great day out with its brilliant playgrounds, obstacle course, Go Ape, maze and gardens.

2

BIRCH

Action-packed itinerary at a hotel that feels like a festival

The story goes that Lady Meux – resident here in the 1880s – transformed the country house estate Birch now occupies into a playground for London's aristocracy, adding a swimming pool and roller skating rink as well as keeping pet zebras in the gardens. In the 1980s, the place was whitewashed into a corporate hotel but fortunately it was eventually reincarnated as Birch, which brought back all the joy. Family fun is at its heart – the main 18th-century red-brick mansion is a labyrinth of corridors with endless things to discover. These range from a pottery studio and interactive bakery to a screening room with deck chairs for watching free family films. Down a long purple corridor, The Hub is a laid-back coworking space with sofas and shared tables, which doubles up as a great place for kids to charge around at the weekend.

Lieutenant Ellis Way, Cheshunt, Goff's Oak,
Waltham Cross EN7 5HW
birchcommunity.com

ROOMS   Birch's aesthetic is one of lively chaos, and their reuse-and-repair philosophy means some corners can feel a little tired at times. There's a sort of minimalist chic to the bedrooms; though sparse (no TVs, fridges, desks) they're welcoming and uncluttered, with giant beds that are great for all piling into. Families are well catered for with options of larger rooms as well as bunk rooms, and bathrooms are a little dated but do the job. A pet peeve for some may be the lack of tea and coffee-making facilities in the rooms, meaning parents on the early shift may have to do it uncaffeinated.

FOOD   With two restaurants, a cafe and a bakery, you won't go hungry. The Zebra Riding Club (a nod to Lady Meux's habit of driving a zebra-drawn carriage) is the most elevated, and embraces open-flame cooking, local suppliers and home-grown produce. Children's menus are available both here and at Valeries, the more relaxed all-day restaurant where you can order breakfast, grilled meat and fish, and seasonal salads. For super-relaxed family dining we love Links Cafe for coffee and breakfast pastries, and pizza on the weekend.

ACTIVITIES   Adults and children are so well provided for with classes, workouts and drop-in sessions that you'll have to craft a careful itinerary for your stay. You can book in to fire your own mugs or try your hand at kneading bread and decorating doughnuts – and little ones are very welcome. There's also a Wellness Centre with spinning and yoga studios, treatment rooms, and restorative workshops such as sound bath healing for adults. Outside, kids can frolic in the lido (though it's not heated so maybe save this for the warmer months), and don't miss the Young Adventurers Club – an outdoorsy corner dedicated to tree climbing and mud pie-making, with forest school sessions on the weekends.

NEARBY   It's more about what's here than what's near, with the huge house and 55 acres of grounds to explore. Saying that, you can connect to London fairly easily: it's a five-minute taxi ride (or 30-minute walk) to Cheshunt station, where you can jump on the overground and be in the City in half an hour.

3

PORT LYMPNE
HOTEL & RESERVE

A sensational safari park stay for budding Attenboroughs

For something a bit different and most definitely memorable, how about sleeping among the lions in an English safari park? Port Lympne is a 600-acre wildlife reserve in Kent, with over 900 animals, from big cats to gorillas, rhinos, giraffes, zebras and monkeys. If you find zoos difficult, you'll be reassured to know profits from the park go towards animal conservation, and it's run in collaboration with The Aspinall Foundation. There are eight sumptuous bedrooms in the Grade II-listed Port Lympne house, but for a more immersive experience families can opt for a bubble pod in the park, a cosy shepherds' hut, self-catering treehouse, or – most exciting of all – a big cat lodge. On-site accommodation comes complete with guided safari truck tours, complimentary golf buddies and access to the park after hours.

Lympne, Nr Ashford, Kent CT21 4PD
aspinallfoundation.org/port-lympne

ROOMS   The premium overnight experiences are the Lion and Tiger Lodges, which have two bedrooms, living spaces and outdoor baths with floor-to-ceiling windows that back onto the big cat enclosures. The Leopard Creek Cabins are also a luxurious option, sleeping four and overlooking the rhino paddock, with outdoor spaces with firepits. For bigger families, the Bear Lodge tents sleep eight, cottage-core Rhino Lodge sleeps five, and the Pinewood Pods (the most wallet-friendly option) sleep four with a double and a bunk bed, shared toilets and communal campfires. If you'd prefer to self-cater, the Treehouses have two bedrooms and spacious kitchenettes.

FOOD   Top-notch dining isn't exactly what you'd expect from a safari park, but you'll be pleasantly surprised with the seven eateries on-site, catering for different palettes and price points. Babydoll's (named after a much-loved gorilla) is great for sourdough pizzas and pasta, and Bear Lodge (open from April to October) is the most relaxed, where you can grab burgers and robata grill dishes to eat while watching the bears.

ACTIVITIES   All overnight stays include a ranger-guided jeep safari that lets families get up-close-and-personal with the animals. Extra hands-on activities can be booked, including a VIP junior ranger tour offering a 'day in the life of a ranger' experience and face-to-face encounters with some of the most endangered species on the planet. There are outdoor play areas and daily keeper talks, and mini monsters will love the Dinosaur Forest with its life-sized sculptures. And if you haven't had enough of wild animals, access to Howletts Wild Animal Park (near Canterbury) is included.

NEARBY   You're a stone's throw from the Kent coast so you can bookend your days with a paddle in the sea. Head for Sunny Sands or Samphire Hoe. Folkestone is only 15 minutes away too, where you can stroll along the Harbour Arm, spot Antony Gormley's *Iron:Man* and scope out the best fish and chips shops. On the edges of town, F51 is a state-of-the-art climbing and skateboarding centre, or for more gentle outdoor family-fun, Brockhill Country Park has scenic walking trails, picnic areas and playgrounds.

4

PORT HOTEL

Stylish and sustainable traditional seaside sojourn

If you're looking to take a seaside family break by train, this is just the ticket. This boutique hotel on the Eastbourne seafront is within walking distance of the station and is great for exploring this stretch of the coast. All the delights of the English seaside are on your doorstep, and while the hotel itself may not be overloaded with family frills, the beachfront location is perfect for popping in and out for naps or forgotten swimming trunks. There are dedicated family rooms, travel cots provided free of charge and room rates that won't break the bank. Introduce the kids to the delights of a traditional British staycation with fish and chips on the promenade, retro arcades on the pier and stunning walks at Beachy Head and Cuckmere Haven. You can even hop on the Coaster bus right outside the hotel and soak up scenic views all the way to Brighton.

11–12 Royal Parade, Eastbourne BN22 7AR
porthotel.co.uk

ROOMS   Bedrooms have a tranquil feel, with tonal palettes, cork floors, and
          sleek wooden headboards. Cots can fit in most of the larger rooms,
          and there are a handful of dedicated family rooms with bunk beds
          or a fold-out sofa bed. If you're able to splurge, it's worth upgrading
          to the Studio Apartment – with more room to spread out, it has an
          XXL-sized bed, sofa, table and chairs, and a spacious terrazzo-clad
          bathroom with a gigantic tub that will fit the whole family. One thing
          to note is that there's no lift here, so you may want to leave the
          pram in the car to save lugging it up and down the narrow stairwell.

FOOD   The restaurant serves dinner from Thursday to Sunday and draws
          in friendly locals on the weekend. They favour local ingredients,
          and weary parents will appreciate the British wines from vineyards
          just a few miles away. During the week, make a beeline for nearby
          family-friendly Qualisea for the best fish and chips in town. The
          hotel serves an à la carte breakfast from 7:30am, with generous
          portions that will fill the hungriest of tums. While there isn't a
          dedicated children's menu, they'll happily dish up half-size
          portions, as well as bite-sized bits for weaning babies, and
          highchairs are available.

NEARBY   The beach is the obvious place to start, followed by the arcades.
          Once you've won a soft toy or two, take a whirl on the Ferris wheel
          or head to the critically acclaimed Towner Gallery with its colour-
          popping façade (keep an eye out for drop-in kids events). If the
          sprogs are up for a walk (or are small enough to be carried), it's a
          beautiful stroll up to Beachy Head or along the meanders at
          Cuckmere Haven. For a change of pace, try the kid-friendly roller
          skating rink. Or, 20-minutes inland (by car), Drusillas Park awaits
          with its wild cats, slides, soft play and Paw Patrol characters. Then
          there's Brighton, just along the coast – a great family day out for
          the price of a bus ticket.

5

THE RETREAT
AT ELCOT PARK

A well-dressed country stay in the North Wessex Downs

This red brick Regency manor is an affordable country escape for guests of all ages, and a particularly charming spot to spend a summer weekend. The lawns are perfect for family garden games, there's an outdoor pool for cooling off, easy countryside rambles from the hotel, and relaxing roll top tubs for slinking into after the kids have gone to bed. Family rooms with bunk beds give you the space and freedom you don't always get with hotels, and the lounges and dining areas on the ground floor feel laid-back and inviting. The interiors are modern vintage, with period features and antique furniture in jewelled paint colours, patterned wallpapers and parasol-striped fabrics. And while some corners might not feel perfectly polished, the affordable room rates are hard to beat.

Elcot, Newbury RG20 8NJ
retreatelcotpark.com

ROOMS   Almost all standard rooms can easily fit an extra cot (£20 per night), and family rooms have bunk beds in a small adjoining room. For even more space, upgrade to the Bushby Bacon suite – one of the hotel's three grand suites – which has lots of floorspace around the four-poster bed (ideal for pushing pram-sized tots to sleep), an adjoining kids' room with bright orange bunk beds, and an XXL-sized family bathroom. All rooms have TVs as well as tea and coffee making facilities, plus raiding rights to the communal pantries, stocked with drinks and snacks.

FOOD   The hotel's main restaurant, 1772, is a classic brasserie serving modern British dishes and Sunday roasts. A children's menu is available, with some adventurous dishes such as parmesan and pea risotto to encourage the tastebuds of burgeoning bon vivants. Yu is a more formal, adults-only pan-Asian restaurant. If you crave a sashimi fix, the hotel can provide baby monitors or a babysitting service. Come morning, breakfast is a modest buffet set-up with a fantastic DIY bacon sandwich station.

ACTIVITIES   Behind the manor, an outdoor heated pool flanked by loungers is the perfect spot to cool off in the warmer months. Kids are welcome to splash around within the dedicated children's times, and there's a daily inflatables hour too. There's a tennis court and an outdoor play area, where giant lawn games like Connect Four, Jenga and croquet provide great family fun, and during school holidays there are often arts and crafts workshops.

NEARBY   Grab a pair of wellies (including little sizes) from the hotel's boot wall and get out into the Kennet Valley. To refuel, Cobbs Farm Shop has a pick-your-own-fruit farm, indoor and outdoor play areas and a cafe. There's a handful of grand historic houses nearby, including the setting of Downton Abbey, Highclere Castle (12 miles away), Shaw House (6 miles) and Blenheim Castle (40 miles). For expending pent-up energy, 4 Kingdoms Adventure Park has oodles to do, and there's also Bucklebury Farm & Safari Park and The Living Rainforest, home to over 850 species of rainforest plants and animals.

6

THE HOXTON, SOUTHWARK

Relaxed, design-led hotel with family-friendly touches

The Hoxton makes travelling to a big city as a family easy, parents don't have to compromise on style, and kids feel well looked after. Southwark is our favourite of the three Hoxton hotels in London, with its spacious rooms, great riverside location and easy transport links with plenty to see and do on the doorstep. The relaxed lobby is somewhere you can hang out without feeling rushed or shushed, and all kinds of children's amenities can be requested for the rooms, from baby baths to bottle warmers. And since timekeeping isn't always top of your mind when travelling with children, we love The Hoxton's 'Flexy Time' policy, which lets you choose your own check in and out times for free when you book direct. So if you're travelling with someone who needs a mid-morning nap that crashes into the standard 11am checkout, you've no need to worry.

40 Blackfriars Road, London SE1 8NY
thehoxton.com/london/southwark

ROOMS   Interiors nod to the neighbourhood's past, once dominated by tanneries and factories. Ranging in size from Shoebox to Biggy, rooms are industrial chic with concrete ceilings, Crittall windows and exposed brick. Babies, toddlers and older kids are all very welcome, with children under 12 sleeping free, and cots or small beds provided on request. With space at a premium in the big city, rooms are on the smaller side (we'd suggest booking at least a Cosy for enough room for a family, and a handful of interconnecting rooms are also available). 'Tiny Hox', a fun partnership with children's brand Smallable, makes parents' lives easier, with baby bath time essentials, nappies, wipes and board games available. A tote bag with a Smallable x Hox colouring book and pencils is also provided for guests aged 0–2.

FOOD   Of the hotel's two dining spots, Albie, the ground floor all-day restaurant, is the most family friendly, serving brunches, salads, burgers and pasta dishes using seasonal ingredients. The relaxed eatery spills out into the lobby and onto a quieter mezzanine, so you can easily commandeer a comfy sofa for an early dinner or leisurely brunch. Room service is also available. Seabird, the hotel's rooftop restaurant, is more of an oysters-and-cocktails destination (with killer views over Southwark), so perhaps one to come back to and enjoy without tiny travellers in tow.

NEARBY   This is a prime location for exploring London: on your doorstep is the South Bank, with all its galleries and arts venues (there's usually something fun going on for kids at the Southbank Centre). The Tate Modern is just a few minutes' walk from the hotel and often hosts great sensory exhibitions for children – not to mention the excellent gift shop, which you'll struggle to leave empty handed. There's also foodie hotspot Borough Market within easy walking distance, and over the bridge in Covent Garden you'll find some of the city's best family-friendly shows.

7

THE GROVE

Five-star family fun on a 300-acre estate

While at first glance this five-star Grade II-listed mansion could seem like a very grown-up stay, with its rolling golf course and sophisticated suites, they've got the luxury family angle down to a tee – so much so that you may never want to leave. There's a solid roster of children's activities on offer here, from archery to tree climbing, falconry and horse riding, and if parents want some peace and quiet there's a kids' club with tons of fun things to do. The five-star hotel marked its 20th anniversary with the opening of the new Bamford spa, a blissed-out spot for parents to make the most of their alone time and experience their own version of R&R. Supersized buffets are available at breakfast and lunch in The Glasshouse restaurant, or there are brasserie-style dishes in The Stables. The only problem is you'll never want to leave.

Chandler's Cross, Watford WD3 4TG
thegrove.co.uk

ROOMS   The 214 rooms are all slick and sophisticated, some with marble-clad bathrooms, others with sweeping views over the estate. Travel cots can be added for free to most rooms, while the deluxe rooms have the most floor space and beds for four. Some of the larger suites also have small kitchens with sinks, fridge-freezers and microwaves, which come in handy for travelling with small children. Baby baths and fluffy baby bathrobes can be added on request.

FOOD   Fill your boots at The Glasshouse, which serves a food hall-inspired international buffet. You'll need deep pockets (though under-threes dine free) but won't need to eat again for a week. At breakfast, choose from pancakes, waffle stacks and elaborate fry-ups. Lunch is everything from sashimi to tandoori chicken cooked to order, roasts with all the trimmings, and fresh pasta made in front of you, so there's sure to be something to please even the pickiest eaters. And the (literal) icing on the cake is a dessert station with a decadent chocolate fondue. For something more straightforward, you can grab a snack or relaxed dinner at The Stables.

ACTIVITIES   In the Walled Garden there's a playground and indoor kids' pool, and there are various free activities on offer in the Potting Shed. Anoushka's Kids' Club is bookable for children aged 2–9, and babysitting is also available if you fancy a few hours to yourselves. Or, head to the outdoor pool and beach if you all want to join in on the fun. There are 300 acres to explore here, and you can pick up a map from reception for the woodland trail. For tired parents, the Bamford spa has treatment rooms, a sauna, steam room and pool will be sure to provide that holiday glow.

NEARBY   Chances are you'll struggle to max out what's on the estate, but if you are itching to get out, the Wizarding World of Harry Potter is a five-minute drive away, the Snow Centre indoor ski slope is a great rainy-day activity, and Whipsnade Zoo is 30 minutes by car. Of course, you've got all of London within reach too, and can take the train from Watford Junction.

8

CABÜ BY THE SEA

Architectural beach shacks by the shore

Inspired by the look of the traditional fishermen's huts at nearby Dungeness, CABÜ by the Sea is a scattering of 13 angular black cabins on a patch of rabbit hole-dotted grassland between Romney Marsh and the English Channel. These sleek, functional cabins are full of cosy home comforts, with separate living spaces that have log burners, TVs and slouchy sofas, and bedrooms with proper beds or bunks. You can whip up one-pot dinners in your own compact kitchen, or fire up the pizza oven for a slice in the Sitooterie, the communal gazebo. Kids can run around freely on the grass, there's a heated outdoor pool that's perfect for sunning and splashing, and only a sea wall separates you from the sandy beach.

Dymchurch Road, St Mary's Bay, New Romney TN29 0HF
holidays.cabu.co.uk/cabu-by-the-sea

ROOMS The glass-fronted cabins come in different shapes and sizes, accommodating between two and six. Wooden interiors bring warmth to the chic furnishings – jute rugs, heavy linen curtains and Loaf sofas. Bathrooms are simple but equipped with power showers and full-length mirrors. Cots can be added to all cabins for £10 per stay. The Boathouse is our top choice for families, with two bedrooms (one with bunks) and a prime position facing the sea.

FOOD Cabins have kitchens with small hobs, fridges and microwave-grills, and the outdoor gas barbecues on the private decks come in handy during the warmer months. The communal Sitooterie, with its benches, gas fires, pizza ovens and festoon lights, is a fun spot to cook or toast s'mores. There's a well-stocked shop at reception that sells freshly baked croissants and coffee, as well as upmarket family-friendly ready meals, chilled English wines, local cheeses, eggs and ice cream, so you can skip the pre-holiday supermarket shop.

ACTIVITIES A heated outdoor pool with loungers is the perfect spot for cooling off, and splashing kids won't be eyeballed. In fact, the floats and goggles in the CABÜ shop encourage the fun. There are a handful of bikes available to borrow, and a few go-karts to pedal around your plot. You'll also find table tennis, traditional wooden lawn games and giant Jenga and Connect Four, and grown-ups can enjoy the outdoor hot tubs and barrel sauna.

NEARBY The sandy shores of St Mary's Bay are perfect for a run around or an evening stroll along the promenade. If you keep walking you'll reach Dymchurch, a sleepy village with a bakery, fish and chip shop and stuck-in-a-time-warp retro arcades. From there you can hop aboard the Romney, Hythe and Dymchurch Railway – a miniature steam train – to Dungeness, a desert-like shingle beach dotted with shipwrecks and artists' cottages. Don't skip Dungeness Snack Shack for the freshest fish and scallop sandwiches, with half-size portions for children.

9

CHEWTON GLEN

Upscale family adventures in an elegant hotel

Located between the Jurassic coast and the New Forest, Chewton Glen is a luxury escape where the whole family will feel pampered. You will eat well and sleep well, and the kids can have a wild time in the treehouse kids' club while you spend quality time in the award-winning spa. The hotel has a feel of old-fashioned elegance, from the first-class service to the handsome lounge bar, manicured croquet lawns and wisteria-clad pergolas, and there are family suites to suit all needs, and even more luxurious treehouses. You're in walking distance of the beach, well placed for exploring the New Forest, and there are plenty of family activities on-site, teddy bear sheep to meet, and a walled kitchen garden where little growers can get their hands dirty.

Christchurch Road, New Milton BH25 6QS
chewtonglen.com

ROOMS   Families can be easily accommodated in the Estate Hotel Rooms, Croquet Lawn Rooms and Junior Suites, where cots and small beds can be added (children stay for free through the school holidays). Upgrade to a luxury Treehouse (fear not, it's glass walled and safe for little crawlers), where kids will love the sense of adventure and hopping in the concierge's buggy over to the restaurant and pool. Breakfast is delivered through a hatch in the wall and can be enjoyed on your own balcony.

FOOD   There are two restaurants on the estate, both of which have excellent kids' menus: The Dining Room is the slightly more formal of the two, with white tablecloths and modern British fare, and The Kitchen, which is a little more laid-back. There's also all-day family-friendly dining in the lounge bar and 24-hour room service. During the school holidays, a buffet supper is served for children between 6-7pm (£10 a head and free for under-fives). The majority of produce comes from the hotel's kitchen gardens or is sourced locally.

ACTIVITIES Whether you want to try new things with the kids or enjoy a little alone time, there are many ways to fill your days. The cookery school is a big hit, with half-day and full-day classes and fun family workshops. Other bookable experiences include foraging, sheep walking, archery and falconry. If you're hoping to tire the kids out for bedtime, there are tennis courts (with private lessons you can book) and an outdoor pool for splashing around. Then there's the Beehive kids' club, where they can spend supervised sessions taking part in arts and crafts or treasure hunts.

NEARBY   It's a lovely walk from the hotel to the beach through the Chewton Bunny Nature Reserve, which opens up onto the sandy shores of Barton-on-Sea, perfect for a paddle or a swim. If you're travelling with toddlers, Paultons Park – home of Peppa Pig World – is a 30-minute drive and a guaranteed hit. There's also Marwell Zoo in Winchester, Monkey World near Wareham, and Exbury Gardens towards Southampton, with beautiful grounds and a family-pleasing steam railway.

10

THREE MILE BEACH

Luxurious beach houses with all the trimmings

Sitting above the sandy dunes of Gwithian Towans, Three Mile Beach is an unbeatable base for sea-centred family fun. Just a five-minute stroll from the shore, there are 15 luxury two, three and four-bedroom beach houses with spacious open plan layouts and private terraces complete with hammocks, hot tubs, barbecues and beanbags. Enclosed spaces mean the kids can safely run around, and while the houses are luxurious, they still have a relaxed surf shack feel and nothing is out of bounds for children. A wide range of extra activities and add-ons, from surfing classes to Ooni pizza ovens, take the hassle out of holidaying here. While there are great sandy beaches on the doorstep, you're only a short drive away from St Ives, with its famous harbour, fishermen's cottages and lively arts scene.

Gwithian Towans, Gwithian, Hayle TR27 5GE
threemilebeach.co.uk

ROOMS   Channelling a surfer's paradise aesthetic, the colourful beach houses have sizeable bedrooms, uncluttered living spaces and cosy reading nooks for kids to discover. Surfboards hang above sliding patio doors, comfy corner sofas swallow you whole, and giant TVs provide rainy day entertainment. Travel cots and highchairs are supplied for free, and a 'Baby Pack' can be booked to help take the pressure off packing, with everything a tiny guest could need – including steriliser, bottle warmer, Nutri-Bullet, baby bath, toilet seat, changing mat and Tupperware.

FOOD   Kitchens are spacious and well-equipped, making cooking here a real joy, and handy flasks and pots are provided for picnics on the beach. An on-site food truck serves fresh salads and light dishes through the summer months, and barista coffees are available from a joyful pink tuk-tuk. For a delicious and interactive family dinner, DIY pizza kits can be booked and delivered to your door, with sourdough balls ready for stretching, tomato sauce and a hamper full of toppings, along with a pizza oven. And if you want a break from cooking or are celebrating something special, private chefs can also be arranged.

ACTIVITIES   Beach time is top of the agenda, with three miles of glorious sandy stretches within a five-minute walk. Surfing is big with guests and locals, and lessons for all ages can be arranged. Mini surfboards, kids' wetsuits and bodyboards are all available to hire, as are standard-size surfboards, stand-up paddle boards, adult wetsuits, coolboxes, parasols and volleyball kits. Yes, they've really thought of everything. On your terrace, you've also got your own sunken hot tub, barrel sauna and gas barbecue, plus hammocks and beanbags for maximum chilling.

NEARBY   St Ives is a 30-minute drive, or you can leave the car at Carbis Bay and walk along the South West Coast Path in about 40 minutes, which is perfect for little hikers, and you can hop on the train on the way back. Also nearby, Godrevy Point peninsula is great for seal spotting (though be wary of steep cliffs), and Trevaskis is a large pick-your-own farm with animals and an excellent farm shop.

11

WATERGATE BAY HOTEL

A surfer's paradise for all ages to enjoy

Set on a two-mile long sandy stretch of coastline just north of Newquay, families feel welcome at Watergate Bay Hotel from the moment they walk in. There are kids wrestling bigger-than-them bodyboards down to the beach, toddlers splashing in the pool and parents jiggling babies in the lobby, hoping the sound of the waves will lull them to sleep. What the hotel may lack in the more personal touches you get from a smaller hotel, it more than makes up for with a raft of parent-pleasing facilities. Along with its brilliant beachside location, pool and plentiful family rooms, there are two free childcare sessions included in your stay. So after unpacking your bags you can hit the spa, have a leisurely lunch, or maybe just read your book in peace while the kids have fun in the Ofsted-rated Kids' Zone.

Watergate Bay Hotel On The Beach,
Trevarrian Hill, Newquay TR8 4AA
watergatebay.co.uk

ROOMS   There are plenty of options for families, from standard doubles (which interconnect) to spacious suites and self-catering apartments. The standard double rooms do work for those with a baby, but can feel like a squeeze once you've unpacked all of the associated paraphernalia, so if you can it's worth sizing up to a family suite. These have a double room (with space for a cot) and bunk beds in a side room. The self-catering apartments have two bedrooms (each with room for a cot or extra bed), plus living and dining areas, kitchenettes and verandas.

FOOD   There are lots of options: The Beach Hut is great for salads, seafood, fish finger sandwiches and burgers (it's our favourite spot and somewhere you can rock up to with sand in your toes); Zacry's is the hotel's main restaurant for the breakfast buffet and brasserie-style dining; and The Living Space is a laid-back lobby set-up with sharing boards and sandwiches. All offer tasty children's menus and highchairs, and the waffle station at breakfast is sure to be a big hit. There's also a handful of shacks between the hotel and beach where you can get coffee, ice creams, cold beers, gourmet hot dogs and pizza.

ACTIVITIES   There's plenty to keep everyone busy. The beach is right outside with bodyboards to hire and surf lessons for all ages in private or group sessions. The Swim Club houses the hotel's indoor pool, a Finnish sauna, hot tub and cafe. Then there's the Kids' Zone, with supervised sessions for children aged from six months to 12 years: nappy changes, feeds, messy arts and craft sessions – they take the whole lot off your hands. In the school holidays, the hotel also hosts forest school-inspired workshops on the beach.

NEARBY   Being on the South West Coast Path, there are easy walks from the doorstep with sea views and great beach stops along the way. 45 minutes away by car, The Lost Gardens of Heligan is a family favourite with its supersized adventure playground, jungle rope bridge, woodland trails, bug hotels, and farm animals. On rainy days, the Eden Project is a winner and The Tide Climbing Centre is excellent for serious scramblers.

12

THE FARM AT AVEBURY

Colourful converted stables in a neolithic landscape

Walking boots at the ready! You're perfectly placed to enjoy a few days out and about in nature here – and if you time your stay right you might snatch a few cuddles with the farm's piglets. Tucked away in a sleepy pocket of Wiltshire, this is the passion-project of Alice and Rob Hues, who've opened the doors of their family farm and transformed the old stables into six charming self-catering stays. Designed with families in mind, stables sleep between two and six (plus room for cot-sized tots), and all open out onto a communal courtyard. Kids will love feeding the lambs, raiding the stack of board games and running free in the courtyard – and there's plenty to see and do on the doorstep, from strolls through Avebury to great pub roasts and walks around UNESCO-rated ancient stone circles.

Galteemore Farm, Beckhampton, Marlborough SN8 1FE
thefarmatavebury.co.uk

ROOMS   The six stables share endorphin-boosting bursts of colour and design ideas you'll want to steal for home: bold panelled feature walls, crimson kitchen cabinets, and geometric Christopher Farr fabrics. In the smaller homes, kitchens are compact but well stocked, while there's more room to spread out in the larger stays. Sleeping arrangements vary, so it's worth checking which works best for you: Windmill Hill has twin beds downstairs (great for kids) and a mezzanine accessed via a steep ladder for grown-ups (less great for tiny tots), while Silbury Hill sleeps six in its three bedrooms. There are highchairs, buggies and baby carriers to borrow, plus functional godsends like blackout blinds and a shared washing machine (handy if you're staying a week).

FOOD   The stables are well set up to self-cater and suit the whole family, with dining tables and highchairs available on request. Should you want to skip the supermarket shop, an extensive choice of farm-to-stable produce is available to pre-order, including eggs, sausages, steaks and bacon, as well as family-friendly homemade dishes like chilli and bolognese, so you can enjoy a night off cooking. Communal Weber barbecues are a fun alfresco dining option too.

ACTIVITIES   It's a working farm so there are always animals around. Alice and Rob regularly rally little guests to tag along on farm feeding duties – giving bottles to the lambs is often a holiday highlight. There's a little wooden playground with swings and a slide that's perfect for blowing off steam, and ride-on cars and diggers dotted around the courtyard to keep little ones busy while you take a breather.

NEARBY   Avebury's ancient stone circle is on the doorstep – one to wow the kids with – and there are rambling routes to suit all ages (download-able route maps are on their website). It's not too long a drive to Lotmead Pick Your Own, Stonehenge, Longleat Safari and the Cotswold Wildlife Park, and you can hide from any rain at Cobbs Farm Shop and Play Barn. There are also plenty of great pubs nearby – we recommend The Red Lion, a picture-perfect thatched pub where kids of all ages are well looked after.

13

MOLLIE'S MOTEL & DINER, BRISTOL

A motorway stopover with style

Don't go expecting grand on-site activities for the kids here (or the parents for that matter) – Mollie's is very much a roadside sleepover, but sometimes that's all you need. Perfect for breaking up long journeys or visiting Bristol on a budget, Mollie's is the motel-offering from the Soho House group. Just off junction 17 of the A4018, it's not the sort of place where you ponder how lovely the setting is, but it feels miles more premium than any other roadside stop, plus there's lots to do nearby. Rooms are sleekly designed and good value with family-friendly bunk rooms sleeping four and make-your-life-easier tech like keyless room access and USB charging ports. Parents will appreciate the Dyson hairdryers, Cowshed products and limitless tea and coffee stations in the lobby, while kids will go wild for the tasty milkshakes in Mollie's Diner.

A4018, Cribbs Causeway, Bristol BS10 7TL
mollies.com

ROOMS There aren't many motels where you'll find terrazzo-clad bathrooms, Hypnos mattresses, velvet armchairs, Cowshed shampoos and rainfall showers. Rooms have a Scandi-ish feel, with light oak and slate finishes, and are as stylish as they are simple. Family rooms have bunk beds the kids will love, while parents will appreciate the giant beds, blackout blinds and limitless coffee – great for those early starts.

FOOD Go in hungry and think about giving the kids their five-a-day some other time. Mollie's is a fun and fast American diner, with double cheeseburgers, hot wings, eggs-all-day and waffles. Saying that, a well-priced menu of kids mini meals (including vegetables) is available from 12pm, and the diner opens from 7am weekdays and 8am on weekends to cater for early birds. Room service is on offer (just order via the Mollie's app), as is bar service if you fancy a Negroni nightcap after a long day in the car.

NEARBY Even though, yes, you're on the edge of a motorway, there's lots to see and do around here. It's just a 15-minute drive to Bristol, or you can hop on the bus that stops outside Mollie's. Two miles down the road is The Wave, a purpose-built inland surfing lake that's perfect for little thrill-seekers. Also on the doorstep is the family-friendly Aerospace Museum, Wild Place Project animal park, and Bristol Activity Centre with paintballing and quad-biking for kids over eight. Should the heavens open and you need somewhere to kill time indoors, you're right opposite the giant Cribbs Causeway retail park – perfect for picking up the raincoats/socks/chargers you invariably left at home.

14

CALCOT & SPA

A country retreat the whole family will love

On first impressions, this honey-hued manor, set just outside
the upmarket town of Tetbury amid the rolling Cotswold hills,
feels like a decidedly grown-up spot. But it's deceptively
brilliant for families. There's a two-storey Playbarn with
supervised sessions, a baby listening service, shaded wooden
playground, outdoor pool, family rooms complete with stair
gates and twin beds – even a dedicated children's teatime that
serves scrummy classics to hungry tots from 5.30pm. Guests
staying in a family room can (and definitely should) take
advantage of the daily complimentary four hours of childcare
in the Ofsted-registered crèche. Rewilding has been a big focus
for the hotel for decades, and you only need step through a
garden gate to be surrounded by wildflowers. The 200-acre
estate has several circular nature trails to follow, depending on
the age and willingness of your little adventurers, plus lovely
big lawns for family games of croquet.

Tetbury, Gloucestershire GL8 8YJ
calcot.co

ROOMS There are 34 rooms and suites across the main house and outbuildings. If you're happy all sleeping in the same room, the Cosy Family Rooms accommodates two adults and two children, while the Comfy Family Rooms and Generous Family Rooms have adjoining kids' rooms with bunk beds. The family suites are split over two floors with a master bedroom, twin room, spacious lounge and private gated gardens. All are stocked with changing mats, bath toys, sterilisers, stair gates, Bramley toiletries, nappy bins and little bathrobes. To save on packing, next-to-me cribs, bouncers, potties and kids cutlery can all be requested.

FOOD All meals are served in the brasserie restaurant overlooking the grounds. There's a dedicated children's teatime from 5:30–6pm, with unfussy classics like spaghetti bolognese on offer, and mini portions of pancakes, eggs, and bacon sandwiches are served up at breakfast. There's a stack of plastic bowls, sippy cups and bibs to borrow too. The hotel offers a baby listening service so you can dine solo, but are more than happy to accommodate highchairs and prams. Room service is also available.

ACTIVITIES The sumptuous spa is a big part of the appeal here, so drop the kids off at the Playbarn, the Ofsted-registered crèche packed with toys, books, arts and crafts, to indulge in some me-time. Older kids will be in their element too, with Nintendo Switch consoles, books, board games, a 12-seater cinema and table football. Guests staying in the family rooms are entitled to up to four hours of childcare a day, and for family time together there's a heated outdoor pool, cargo bikes, tennis courts, an outdoor mud kitchen and walking trails through the Cotswold countryside.

NEARBY The grand town of Tetbury (King Charles lives down the road) is a few minutes' drive, where, nestled among the high-end antique shops, you'll find a handful of bakeries and family-friendly pubs. Westonbirt National Arboretum is a 10-minute drive and is a fun family day out for all ages. The forest has towering trees from all over the world, the Zog activity trail, with giant Gruffalo sculptures to spot, as well as a woodland play area and a treetop walkway.

15

ST. ENODOC HOTEL

Slow days by the sea in a gracious coastal hotel

Five minutes' stroll from Rock and a breathtaking walk along the coast path to Polzeath, St. Enodoc Hotel is brilliantly placed for sandy summer holidays. Kids can be in and out of the waves all day, there are plenty of cafes, pubs and pasty shops for picnics and easy family meals, and all ages feel well catered for. None more so than parents, who, thanks to the spacious two-bedroom family suites can relax in their own room after a day of sandcastle building, or, alternatively, nab a table at the beautiful restaurant terrace and watch boats bob on the Camel Estuary. There's a swimming pool in the impressive cottage-core gardens, a delicious children's menu in the restaurant, a games room with colouring books, toys and table football, and cheery staff for whom nothing seems too much trouble.

Rock Road, Rock, Wadebridge PL27 6LA
enodoc-hotel.co.uk

ROOMS   There are 17 rooms and four suites. The spacious Family Suites have two bedrooms (one with twin beds), a small but functional kitchenette and a family bathroom. They're not designed with self-catering in mind but offer some flexibility, with a microwave and kids' plates and cutlery coming in handy for mini mealtimes and snacks. Thoughtful parent-pleasing touches include blackout blinds, Bramley's Little B products in the bathroom, baby monitors to borrow and babysitting services, and there are Yoto Players with a folder full of stories and songs.

FOOD   There are two restaurants in the hotel: St. Enodoc Brasserie is a relaxed dining room with amazing views and a terrace, and Karrek is an intimate white-tableclothed tasting-menu restaurant that showcases the best of Cornwall. Naturally, the Brasserie is the best for families. Dinner is served from 6pm, and a short but sweet children's menu features fresh grilled fish and macaroni cheese, while adults can tuck into two- or three-course set menus as well as local oysters and wines. Breakfast is served in the same space, with à la carte options included in room rates.

NEARBY   Just five minutes from the hotel, you can hop on the ferry to cross over the estuary to Padstow. Little ones love the adventure, and the ferries regularly run all day with no need to book ahead. There, the Camel Valley Trail is a flat cycling route that runs 18 miles along a disused railway line through scenic countryside. You can hire bikes (for all ages), bike seats and trailers in Padstow and pootle along at your leisure. For a smaller adventure, Rock Beach is just 10 minutes from the hotel and is perfect for sandcastles and swimming, and Polzeath – one of Cornwall's most beloved wide sandy beaches – is a must-go. It's just over an hour's walk along the coast path (though it's quite undulating so little legs might need a break here and there), and its gentle waves and rock pools make it great for paddling, body-boarding and beginner surf lessons. If you've all had enough beach time, Eden Project is always a big hit, only 45 minutes away by car.

16

LAKES BY YOO

Luxury lakeside lodges that you'll never want to leave

Somewhere to push the boat out (quite literally), this is a luxury retreat near the picture-perfect villages of Burford and Lechlade-on-Thames, where you can enjoy family time in style. The 800-acre estate is home to 100 or so private lakeside holiday homes, and a handful of rentable villas and apartments that make for soul-restoring stays. In summer, spend long days lounging by the lake, and in the colder months, sink into the sofa by the fire after rosy-cheeked walks and hearty pub lunches. Nothing's too much to ask for here, and private chefs and mixologists-by-the-hour can be booked, as well as in-room facials, and babysitters. Given the lakeside location, this is a great break for those with babes-in-arms and older children – less so the crawling kind.

High Street, Lechlade GL7 3DT
thelakesbyyoo.com

ROOMS   The super-luxe villas feature giant comfy sofas, log burners, thick rugs, spa-like bathrooms, and beautiful views across the water. With king-size everything (rooms, beds, bathtubs, balconies), there's plenty of space to spread out here, with different sized villas and apartments to suit 4–10 guests. Those putting little ones to bed will appreciate the separate spaces and soundproofed bedrooms, which mean you can enjoy a late dinner on the balcony or TV in the lounge without having to keep the noise down.

FOOD   With your own private residence, you're in charge of cooking, and the compact but high-spec kitchens make light work of that. Enjoy family lunches and dinners around the elegant dining table or out on your lakeside terrace. Should you want a break from cooking, private chefs are on hand (at a cost) to prepare family feasts, and back in the real world there's also Elsa's cafe, a tipi serving kid-friendly burgers and brunches.

ACTIVITIES   For such a sophisticated spot, children are impressively well catered for. There's an indoor pool (great for rainy days), playground and zip wire to keep little ones entertained, plus activities, electric bikes and water sports for older kids. We recommend trying to snatch an hour to yourself and booking into one of the new treatment rooms for a massage, and – should you be able to cash in on more 'me-time' while you're here – there's a gym, yoga classes, sauna and steam room.

NEARBY   You can easily keep yourselves entertained on this 850-acre estate, but nearby Burford is worth a visit and regularly ranks as one of the most picturesque villages in England. What it lacks in children's entertainment, it makes up for in premium deli produce for gourmet picnics. For animal encounters, Cotswold Wildlife Park is a 15-minute drive away with its giraffes and big cats. It's also worth keeping an eye on Lake By Yoo's website for local listings, since there's always something happening in the Cotswolds, from farmers markets to local fairs, fairgrounds and air shows.

17

THE BULL INN

Sustainable stay with beaches and rambles in all directions

Few places in the UK can put a spring in your step and give you a renewed sense of community spirit quite like Totnes, and The Bull is the best base for enjoying it. It defines itself as 'radically ethical', committed to doing good for the community and the planet, and a stay here is a glorious way to give the kids a lesson in treading lightly on the Earth. Founded by a veteran environmentalist, their 'no-Bull rules' govern how they run the business, and you'll find everything here is painstakingly considered – from the food suppliers for the veg-heavy menus to their low-intervention wine list, pre-loved furniture, locally made bathroom tiles, organic bed linens and solar panel-heated hot water. They offer all guests a 10 per cent discount for travelling via train – an added incentive for parents tired of the screaming from the back seats.

102 High Street, Rotherfold, Totnes TQ9 5SN
bullinntotnes.co.uk

ROOMS   The decor embraces the quirks of the 18th-century inn – original beams and all. Rooms are light and bright with lime-plastered walls, reclaimed furniture, reworked vintage fabrics, organic linens, handmade bathroom tiles and locally sourced bath products. The pub itself has nine rooms, most of which can fit a cot or trundle bed, but our favourite for families is The Albatross, a four-bed apartment across the street that offers more space and the freedom to self-cater. There you'll find kings and super-kings with room for cots, two bathrooms, a modern kitchen, a cosy lounge with a projector for movie nights, and a private roof terrace where kids can play outside while you enjoy a morning coffee.

FOOD   The kitchen is the beating heart of the pub and meals here are a real joy. The dining room is spacious and super-relaxed, with prams, highchairs and children crawling under tables all commonplace. Menus change daily with organic ingredient-led seasonal dishes using produce from honest, local and fairtrade suppliers. Dishes feel creative but not overdone, working hard to showcase unsung ingredients, and portions are fairly priced and well-sized. Though there's no dedicated children's menu, the kitchen is always happy to adapt dishes and plate up mini portions.

NEARBY   Sandwiched between the coast and Dartmoor National Park, you've got ready-made family days out all around, from nature rambles and beach days to crabbing at Brixham or water sports in Torquay. Totnes is perfect for pottering, a warren of charming streets with independent stores selling local arts and crafts, and Leechwell Community Gardens is an unexpected gem in the middle of town with a wooden playground and picnic areas. There's also Steamer Quay play park, a ship-themed playground that young explorers will love to clamber around, or you can hop aboard the South Devon Railway, a steam train that chuffs from Totnes to Buckfastleigh through the scenic River Dart Valley. It's only half an hour each way and is a great rainy-day jaunt. And 15 minutes away, Pennywell Farm will delight younger kids with micro pigs, tractor rides, a miniature railway, a maze, soft play and a cafe.

18

CARBIS BAY
HOTEL & ESTATE

A luxury hotel with its own Blue Flag beach

Easily one of the most tropical spots in Britain with its white sands and sparkling sea, under blue skies Carbis Bay is a dead ringer for the Caribbean. The luxurious hotel was built in 1894 for the tourism boom that came with the introduction of the railway line, and has since been extended with cottages, sea-view suites and ultra-luxe beachfront lodges. This is a great central base for exploring Cornwall, with easy walks along the South West Coast Path and St Ives just a 25-minute stroll away (and if little legs get tired, just hop on the train for a scenic journey back). The beach outside is a fantastic sheltered swimming spot, from where you can often spot seals, and the hotel has a pool, spa, several restaurants, a kids' club and babysitting services.

Carbis Bay, St. Ives TR26 2NP
carbisbayhotel.co.uk

ROOMS   In the main Victorian house, rooms and suites feel traditional; some have balconies or garden patios, and all can accommodate a cot or a child's bed. The most luxurious accommodations are the beachfront lodges, should you be lucky enough to afford them (they go from £1,500 a night, but what you save on *not* flying to the Caribbean, you might want to splurge here!). They sleep six, with three-storey living spaces, hot tubs on private terraces and direct beach access. For something more achievable but still very special, the cottages and apartments are great for families, with plenty of room to spread out and self-cater.

FOOD   With four restaurants on site, you're spoilt for choice. The Beach Club is the obvious option for families, set just back from the sand and serving all-day pizzas, salads and seafood, with a reasonably priced children's menu. For coffees and snacks The Deli is an easy grab-and-go option. Or, if you want to push the boat out, Ugly Butterfly offers a five- or seven-course tasting menu – and little gourmands needn't miss out as there's a five-course tasting menu for kids, too. The hotel also offers hampers packed with fresh Cornish produce for beach picnics, so you've no need to wrestle toddlers out of their swimmers for lunch.

ACTIVITIES   A kids' club runs through the school holidays (there's a daily charge of £30 per child), with activities such as crafting mosaics, pizza making, face painting and beach sessions, and includes a take-home gym bag, sun cap and water bottle. Paddleboards and canoes can be hired from the beach, and the hotel will happily arrange family outings and boat trips. For parents, there's yoga, a gym, and a spa that offers everything from gel manicures to deep tissue massages.

NEARBY   St Ives is a short walk along the coastal path, where you can potter around the tiny streets, enjoy more beach fun (there are seven within walking distance), visit the Tate, and get Cornish pasties from St Ives Bakery for lunch. Newquay's Blue Reef aquarium is a perfect rainy-day spot, while thrill-seekers should make a beeline for Flambards Theme Park, with its sky-high rides and life-size dinosaurs.

19

THE BRADLEY HARE

Relaxed, design-led hostelry for exploring the West Country

Standing proud in the sleepy hamlet of Maiden Bradley, The Bradley Hare is a handsome village pub with rooms that's well placed for visiting favourite family day trip destinations such as Longleat Safari and Stonehenge. This is a relaxed spot in an upmarket part of the country (the village is within the Duchy of Somerset estate), but as sophisticated as it feels, children from tots to teens are welcomed with all smiles from the staff. Days here are designed to begin at a leisurely pace (as much as they ever can with kids in tow) with tea in bed and unhurried breakfasts. Nearby, there are grand Palladian villas to admire, stone circles to marvel at, safari parks to delight, and the gorgeous West Wiltshire Downs and Cranborne Chase to roam.

Church Street, Maiden Bradley, Warminster BA12 7HW
thebradleyhare.co.uk

ROOMS The 12 rooms are set across the pub and the adjacent coach house, and all are beautifully appointed by a former Soho House design director. Painted in serene Farrow & Ball greens and greiges, with antiques, upholstered headboards, goose down duvets and Burlington bedecked bathrooms, you definitely won't feel like you're sacrificing stylish surrounds for a family-friendly stay. Most rooms will fit a cot (travel cots are provided free of charge), but those in the Coach House are best for families as they're slightly larger and can accommodate an additional futon. There are also two rooms in the main house that can be interconnected if you'd like a little more space.

FOOD Mealtimes here are a real treat, with beautifully cooked dishes elevated far above the usual pub fare. Menus feel modern and seasonal, and it's nice to see kids' menus that are not too far removed from the adult offering. If it's cold and blustery, hunker down in a cosy corner by the open fire, and in warm weather dining in the garden is a delight – with the added bonus that kids can run around without getting underfoot. If you'd prefer an adults-only dinner once the kids are in bed, baby monitors can be provided. Breakfast is served from 8am to 11am and is a short menu of well-done classics. And while it's not technically part of the pub, the kids will love the milk-dispensing hut next door, with sugary syrup dispensers for DIY milkshakes.

NEARBY Bruton and Frome are among the nearest towns, with their independent boutiques, artisan coffee shops and flea markets. You're close to the famous landscaped gardens of Stourhead estate, and Longleat Safari Park, a monster of a fun day out, is 10 minutes away: there's the safari drive-through as well as meerkats, monkeys and otters to get close to, plus rides, a maze, an adventure play-ground and the Elizabethan mansion and gardens to explore. If awe and wonder are higher on the agenda, historic Stonehenge is a 30-minute drive, and there are ample walking routes around here too.

20

ARTIST RESIDENCE, BRISTOL

Hip home from home, perfect for exploring the West Country

An old boot factory turned buzzy boutique hotel, Artist Residence is a great base for exploring Bristol as a family, with its relaxed, friendly feel, spacious rooms and excellent location in the creative St Pauls neighbourhood. Bringing both style and substance, the Georgian townhouse has been transformed into a welcoming city retreat with local art on display, raw plaster walls, and a homely mix of vintage and contemporary furniture. The all-day restaurant and lounge are spaces where you can linger and not have to worry about spreading out or making a bit of a mess. The kids won't feel out of place lounging on the comfy shabby-chic sofas, there's a ping-pong table and courtyard garden and don't leave before getting a fun family portrait in the retro photobooth.

28 Portland Square, St Paul's, Bristol BS2 8SA
artistresidence.co.uk

ROOMS   Of the 23 rooms and suites, 13 are suited for young families with extra floor space for a cot, and there are three rooms that can fit a cot *and* a small bed. Interiors feel bohemian and have a deliberately unpolished finish, which makes it much easier to relax when travelling with kids. That's not to say it doesn't feel considered, and there's plenty for parents to love here: luxury roll top baths, fluffy robes, Bramley products in the bathrooms, rainfall showers and minibars stocked with local craft beers and gin.

FOOD   Boot Factory, the all-day kitchen, is spread across the library, cafe and snug, with a super-relaxed and welcoming vibe throughout. Grab a spot on the sofa by the fireplace, a window seat in the corner, or take over a leather booth. The breakfast menu has everything from Turkish eggs to pancake stacks, and marvellously melty cheese toasties are a highlight at lunch. Dinners using seasonal ingredients are served in the private dining room, but if you're on the early bedtime shift, sharing plates, pizzas and cocktails make for a quick and low-key snack in the bar. Highchairs and a kids' menu are available.

NEARBY   This is a great city for a family trip (though little legs may complain about its many hills), and you're perfectly positioned for exploring Stokes Croft and Montpelier – creative neighbourhoods brimming with independent stores and artisan cafes (they're no stranger to a babyccino around here). St Paul's Adventure Playground is right around the corner from the hotel and is a brilliant community-run playground for kids of all ages. On the other side of the river, Windmill Hill City Farm is a family favourite, and since climbing is so popular around these parts why not start them young at Clip 'n' Climb, an excellent all-ages indoor climbing centre. Bristol is a proudly sustainable city so it's easy to holiday here without a car, and Artist Residence is just a 20-minute stroll from Bristol Temple Meads station.

21

MOONFLEET MANOR

All the family activities you could wish for in one place

Overlooking Chesil Beach on Dorset's dramatic Jurassic Coast, Moonfleet Manor is a newly renovated country house with family frills aplenty. There are room options to suit all set-ups, extremely family-friendly dining, a milk butler and children's facilities that are exhausting to recount, let alone engage in. There's a science room full of wacky experiments to try, a climbing wall, skittles alley, retro arcade games, crazy golf, indoor and outdoor pools, and even an escape room experience that older kids will love. Kids can borrow bedtime stories from the dedicated children's library, and you can take advantage of the baby monitoring service to sip a cocktail on your own sea-view terrace or in the bar. All this plus 90 minutes of complimentary childcare each day. Our bags are packed.

Fleet Road, Weymouth DT3 4ED
moonfleetmanorhotel.co.uk

ROOMS   The hotel is designed with families in mind, so even their entry-level rooms can comfortably fit a couple and a cot. The deluxe rooms and family suites can sleep two adults and two children in separate rooms, and a few suites sleep six. Some rooms offer sea views, others have original timber beams and modern four-poster beds. Bathrooms are stocked with Little B by Bramley toiletries for kids, and all have tubs. Packing for a stay here is a breeze since they can provide all the essentials – just let them know in advance what you need and they'll get it ready.

FOOD   Breakfast is a buffet and, given that pretty much all the guests have children, you don't have to worry about yours running amok. Early dinners are available from 5pm, and there's a lengthy children's menu, plus the kitchen is happy to whip up half-portions of adult dishes. There's even a purée menu for weaning tots. But our favourite thing has to be the milk butler – room service deliveries of warm bottled milk for morning feeds and milky cuddles.

ACTIVITIES   There's plenty to keep all ages entertained. Tots from three months to eight years can be dropped off at the Four Bear's Den Ofsted-registered crèche, where they can get messy with face painting, arts and crafts and outdoor activities. For family time together there are swimming pools, tennis courts, a cinema with daily screenings, guided fossil walks, crazy golf, a race-the-clock escape room and an all-new science room. If you're wondering when the parents get to relax, there's a spa for top-to-toe pampering.

NEARBY   You'll struggle to tear yourselves away, but there's plenty more to see nearby. You're only five miles from Weymouth, a quintessential British seaside resort with its sandy beach and promenade. On rainy days you can take cover in the Sea Life Adventure Park, a full day out in itself, with penguins, play areas and a slide 'n' splash pool. Durdle Door, a huge natural limestone arch, is a must-see while you're in Dorset – the beach is a bit of a trek down but worth it for the wow factor and the fossil hunting.

22

TREDETHICK FARM COTTAGES

Self-catering stays designed around children

There are some places that just happen to work well for families. Then there are others, like Tredethick, that were set up with families in mind from the start. This cluster of colourful cottages on a Cornish farm is surrounded by pigs, ponies, hens and goats, and has an indoor play barn, heated pool, an outdoor balance bike track, tractor rides, a wooden playground, a maze, a football pitch... the list goes on. Parents will love how much there is to entertain the kids (including rainy-day contingencies), the parenting paraphernalia provided (sterilisers, stair gates, the works) and that there are beaches, towns, castles, ice cream stops and cycle trails all within a 20-minute drive. If kids were booking the holiday, this is where they'd choose.

Lostwithiel, Cornwall PL22 OLE
tredethick.com

ROOMS   The eight cottages are equally family-friendly but vary in size, offering 1–3 bedrooms and sleeping up to seven. Bright, mood-boosting interiors promise to lift you up, while kids rooms are sweet with animal-printed curtains, teddies and bedtime books. Every little touch considers tiny guests, from the bed guards, blackout blinds and night lights to highchairs and stair gates so parents can rest easy. Each cottage has its own private garden and BBQ for laid-back family feasts outside.

FOOD   It's all self-catering so you've got plenty of flexibility, and kitchens are well-stocked with plastic cutlery and crockery. There's a small but jam-packed farm shop on-site that's open 24/7, where you can pick up pantry essentials along with locally sourced sausages and bacon, COOK frozen ready meals, and (depending on your parenting style and level of desperation) perfect toddler bribing fodder like ice lollies and fudge.

ACTIVITIES   Whatever the weather, there's plenty to keep all ages busy. Outdoors, there's a playground, farm trail and farm-themed balance bike track, plus a host of animals to meet and ponies to ride. The indoor soft play is a godsend on rainy days (complete with newspapers and coffee to keep grown-ups happy), and the indoor pool is heated to a toasty 30 degrees – ideal for giving water babies their first dip – and swim lessons can be arranged. Is it bedtime yet? After all that fun, parents can hide in the hot tub garden and unwind.

NEARBY   As if there wasn't enough to keep you busy on site, there's also plenty to see and do in the area. You can take your pick of Cornwall's best beaches, family favourites like the Eden Project and Lost Gardens of Heligan are within a 20-minute drive, and Thomas the Tank Engine fans won't want to miss the Bodmin & Wenford Steam Railway. Fowey is a nice day out with its eateries (North Street Kitchen is an excellent laid-back lunch spot), pubs and shops, and the sheltered Readymoney Cove has a pontoon for swimming out to. Older kids and adults can try paddleboarding lessons on the Fowey Estuary.

23

FOWEY HALL

A seaside stay designed with family fun in mind

If you're looking for a family holiday where everyone feels thoroughly catered for, Fowey Hall is hard to beat. There are indoor and outdoor pools for swimming laps and splashing on inflatables, a children's library with daily story time, play areas, woodland trails, a family-friendly spa, a great nearby beach, baby monitoring available in every room, a milk butler who'll drop off bedtime bottles, and a joyful 90 minutes of complimentary daily childcare included. You can pack light and leave most of the parenting baggage at home because they've got everything covered here, from bibs to travel cots. Fowey itself is perfectly sized for strolling around, with plenty of relaxed restaurants and pubs, and it's a lovely pram-friendly walk from the hotel down to Readymoney Cove.

Hanson Drive, Fowey, Cornwall PL23 1ET
foweyhallhotel.co.uk

ROOMS   All rooms are set up to accommodate families both big and small, and include natural toiletries, robes, slippers and 50-inch TVs. Those travelling with babies and tots in cots can comfortably fit into a Classic Sea View Room, or if you want a bit more space but are all happy to bed down in the one room, Deluxe Rooms sleep two adults and two children. For extra freedom or a special treat, the suites have multiple bedrooms and can sleep up to five.

FOOD   Mealtimes are flexible, seasonal Cornish produce is championed, and there's a special kids' dinner service from 5–6pm each day with menus full of healthy, varied options. If you're dining once the little ones are in bed or fancy a drink at the bar, a video monitoring service is available and babysitters can also be arranged. A purée menu is offered for weaning babies, though the kitchen is happy to blitz up pretty much anything off the menu.

ACTIVITIES   Kids as young as three months can be dropped off at the Ofsted-registered Four Bears' Den, with dressing-up boxes, arts and crafts and messy play. Up to 90 minutes of supervised childcare is included in each day of your stay, so take advantage and book yourself a spa treatment. The heated outdoor pool has sea views, and armbands, floats and noodles are supplied. There are vintage arcade games and table football in the games room, but if you prefer the kids to be out in the fresh air there's a *Wind in the Willows*-inspired outdoor play area with a zip line, swings and Toad Hall playhouse.

NEARBY   If you prefer beaches to pools, it's a scenic (and pram-friendly) walk from the hotel down to Readymoney Cove, a sheltered cove with a pontoon for swimming out to. Wellies, fishing nets, buckets and spades can all be borrowed from the hotel. It's a short drive to Lost Gardens of Heligan, which often hosts pop-up seasonal events featuring favourite book characters, and the Eden Project is only 20 minutes away, too. Fowey Hall also has a great calendar on their website highlighting family-friendly events, so it's worth checking what's on while you're here.

24

HOPE COVE HOUSE

A family-run seaside stay with foodie credentials

For a relaxed break making memories by the sea, Hope Cove House is just the place. This seaside house has been lovingly transformed into a beautiful foodie-focused boutique hotel that overlooks a quiet sandy cove on the south Devon coast. Excellent eats include freshly caught fish on the BBQ, homemade pasta and colourful salads using homegrown produce. The owners have young kids of their own so they know what works, and thoughtful touches like a crate of Lego in the lounge and bedtime books make families feel very welcomed. You're right on the South West Coast Path and it's just a five-minute walk to the village and 15 minutes to Salcombe. The sandy beach of Inner Hope is a blissful quiet spot, perfect for long lazy days making sandcastles, skimboarding and playing in the waves.

Inner Hope, Kingsbridge TQ7 3HH
hopecovehouse.co

ROOMS   Of the nine bedrooms, there are two family rooms that can sleep broods of four and five, and the rest are doubles or twins which can all accommodate cots or small beds. Being a guest here feels like staying with a close relative who has really good taste: there's Aesop soap in the bathrooms, soft bed linens and sea views in place of screens. While there are certainly no garish nautical themes, the calming decor feels inspired by the ocean.

FOOD   The food is the major draw. The short, unfussy dinner menu changes each day to take advantage of the best available seasonal ingredients, so you could stay for a week and not tire of eating here. In winter, enjoy dramatic views through picture windows, and in summer it's a treat to eat al fresco family meals on the terrace. Kids are well looked after, with children's menus and highchairs available. A continental breakfast is included in the rates, and bacon sandwiches and eggs can be made to order.

NEARBY   Through the summer months, you won't want to do anything other than enjoy the brilliant beaches around the hotel. Inner Hope is calm and perfect for little paddlers, and Mouthwell has a lifeguard on duty through the summer months. Hope Cove, a traditional fishing village, is a five-minute stroll along the coastal path and has some charming eateries and pubs. For more bustle, the popular resort town of Salcombe is a 15-minute drive away. A fun family day out starts with ice creams from Salcombe Dairy and ends with a boat trip over to East Portlemouth.

25

HAWARDEN ESTATE

A campsite with a difference for budding explorers

If you're looking for something between camping and glamping, Hawarden is just the place. Located just within the border of North East Wales, it's a 26-pitch campsite that's open from May to August, and has lots of amenities on-site including a farm shop, bakery, pub and deli, so you don't feel totally removed from creature comforts. Founded and run by the Good Life Society (also the brains behind Glen Dye Cabins & Cottages, no.29), everything about it feels family orientated and fun – from the summer toddler club to the pick-your-own-fruit field. If, even with all the on-site facilities, you'd rather glamp than camp, you can opt for one of the pre-erected bell tents so you can jump straight into holiday mode and don't have to argue over who left the tent poles at home.

Hawarden Estate, Flintshire CH5 3FB
hawardenestate.co.uk

ROOMS   With only 26 pitches on 6.5 acres, there's ample space to spread
out and you'll never feel on top of your neighbours. There are 12
bring-your-own tent pitches, three bring-your-own van pitches, and
11 pre-erected bell tents that sleep two adults and two children –
three of which have their own fire pits and outdoor chairs. Toilet
and shower blocks are shared facilities, as are the outdoor kitchens,
barbecues and dining areas, which are all child-friendly and very
well maintained.

FOOD   The Hawarden Estate Farm Shop is at the heart of the campsite
and is a cafe-come-deli-come-artisan bakery with a bustling
atmosphere, helpful staff and family-friendly dining room full of
colourful tables and fridges overflowing with organic vegetables,
local beers and homemade sweet treats. Open for breakfast, lunch
and dinner, menus change daily and use locally sourced and
seasonal produce. If you'd prefer to self-cater, food hampers can
be ordered from the farm shop too – ideal for low-key family feasts
that are fun for aspiring chefs to get involved in preparing.

ACTIVITIES   The lake is open for swimming on certain days, there are wooden
playgrounds to burn off steam, table tennis, and musical trumpets
in the forest. The Explorer's Trail is a signposted nature ramble
that all ages will enjoy, just pick up an activity pack from the farm
shop and follow the orange arrows into the wood, ticking off sights
and activities as you go. There's also the Explorer Club, craft and
play sessions for mini adventurers that take place most Saturdays,
and forest school-style activities through the school holidays.

NEARBY   The Boardroom climbing centre, just five minutes away, is great
for all ages. There's Beeston Castle for a walk through history,
Chester Zoo, and Chester itself has plenty for families: walk along
the Roman walls, hop on a river boat, and stop off at Storyhouse
for relaxed dining, family shows and a kids library to browse. Then
there are the mountainous national parks and beaches of north
Wales, Llandudno is a 45-minute drive, and Colwyn Bay a little
closer – where you can swim, see rare animals at the conservation
zoo, and take a tram up the Great Orme.

26

FFOREST FARM

If you like forest school, you'll love Fforest Farm

Fforest is a mini empire of hospitality spots in Pembrokeshire which are known for their stunning locations, great food and unique accommodation. At their heart, these holiday homes strive to connect people with nature for wholesome family staycations. Our favourite, Fforest Farm, is a bit like a toppled over hotel, with Japanese-inspired geodomes, canvas bell tents and cabin-like shacks made from reclaimed materials set upon 200 leafy acres and sandwiched between the sea and the heritage town of Cardigan. There's an on-site micro-pub, a shop where you can buy locally churned butter and Fforest's own seaweed-infused gin, and a calendar of activities through the school holidays. Kids will love running barefoot in nature, while parents will love that it's just 20 minutes' drive from the beach and so relaxed that it doesn't matter if (or when) the kids go a bit feral.

Cwm Plysgog, Cardigan, Cilgerran SA43 2TB
coldatnight.co.uk/fforest-farm

ROOMS   From bannisters made from driftwood to Welsh blankets, there's authenticity and craftsmanship in every aspect of Fforest. There are eight different accommodation options, all of which have their own kitchens, with the Crog Lofts being a favourite for families with its double beds on a mezzanine and bunk beds on the ground floor. They've got outdoor kitchens under sheltered porches, and cosy indoor living areas that open onto communal green space. Interiors are simple but stylish, with mid-century furniture and slate floors with toasty underfloor heating.

FOOD   From November until March, all stays are self-catering. Y Bwthyn, the cosy candle-lit micro-pub, is open from the Easter holidays until October half term, and breakfast is served through the school holidays, as are Saturday night suppers. Pizzatipi, also by Fforest, is ideal for early family dinners. It's a relaxed outdoor eatery set on the riverside in Cardigan (five minutes' drive) and serves stonebaked pizzas and Welsh craft beers.

ACTIVITIES   If your kids love forest school, they're going to be in their element, building fires, cooking outdoors, canoeing along the Teifi Gorge and wandering woodland trails. There are kids' workshops and family activities through the school holidays, and during term time kayaks and canoes can be hired nearby, and the team can point you in the direction of bikes, hikes and surfing lessons. After a day chasing little ones around, grown-ups will appreciate sinking into Fforest's cedar barrel sauna.

NEARBY   The beaches of West Wales are close by – Mwnt is one of the best, a secluded bay with soft waves (great for bodyboarding) and a hill for seal and dolphin watching, and has parking, toilets and a snack kiosk, making it an easy day out. For younger kids, Folly Farm (and zoo) is fun, and there's also a play barn and adventure playground – good for wet days. Ten minutes away, Dyfed Horse Riding Centre leads riding trails through the wooded valleys. The town of Cardigan is a 40-minute drive and has charming delis and bakeries – the artisan doughnuts at Crwst are a particular highlight.

27

MILOVAIG HOUSE

Find your spirit of adventure in the Scottish Isles

Forget Baby Shark and Cocomelon. Here, the kids only have to press their little noses up against the enormous floor-to-ceiling windows overlooking the water to be entertained, with the Inner Hebrides' wild beauty in full force. Eagle-eyes might spot whales and dolphins from the house, and closer by there are grazing sheep. After bedtime, parents can savour the starriest of skies from the wood-fired hot tub, and, if lucky, catch a glimpse of the Northern Lights. This remote holiday haven is somewhere to hone kids' adventurous spirit, spending long days outdoors and leisurely evenings telling stories around the firepit. Serene, stripped-back interiors echo the remote landscape and allow plenty of floor space for kids to sprawl. Peeling yourself away to go home is the hard part.

16 Lower Milovaig, Isle of Skye IV55 8WR
sandandstoneescapes.com

ROOMS The 19th-century crofter's house has been beautifully renovated, with soft Nordic-inspired interiors and huge windows to bring the outside in. There are two king-size rooms on the first floor, one with twin beds which works well for kids. Cots can be added for the littlest of guests, and the sofa bed in the downstairs snug can also accommodate an adult or two children. On the ground floor, there's room to spread out with a dining room, snug, sunroom and kitchen. In summer, the light late evenings should be savoured outdoors, and in winter, snuggle in with the log burner roaring and savour the views while the kids raid the basket of toys and games.

FOOD It's all self-catering, which allows for maximum flexibility, whether the kids are eating with you or not. Parents will be pleased to find a highchair as well as children's plates and cutlery in the kitchen, which is well-sized and well-equipped. Pick up the catch of the day from local fishermen at Meanish Pier, a five-minute walk away, and cook the freshest of simple suppers on the firepit. Don't forget to drop by Cafe Lephin, a family-run cafe just a couple of miles down the road in Glendale, for homemade cakes.

NEARBY There are family-friendly walks from the doorstep, which allow you to fully experience the stunning scenery the Isle of Skye is famed for. Varkasaig Beach is only 12 miles down the road: a shimmering black sand beach that is gentle for swimming – and kids will be delighted by the cows that roam on the sands. Dunvegan Castle is a 30-minute drive and has plenty to entertain curious kids, from the Wild Wood Trail to seal-spotting trips out on the loch (free for under-fives), as well as family workshops and activities throughout the school holidays.

28

THE WOODLAND COTTAGES

Cosy boltholes among the mountains and moorlands

You won't have to worry about screentime here, as your days will be spent immersed in nature. There are hills to climb, lochs to swim in, dens in the trees, a garden to run around barefoot, red squirrels and deer to get acquainted with – and even a zip wire on the lawn. This cluster of handsome stone-walled cottages are set on three acres of shared gardens in the Abernethy Forest, just a kissing gate away from the Cairngorms National Park. Borrow bikes and take in Scotland's breathtaking mountains, moorlands, forests and rivers, then stop for a picnic in the hills and toast marshmallows together over a campfire. The cottages have a clean Scandi-feel and thoughtful comforts, but they remain somewhere to enjoy the simpler things in life.

Dell Road, Nethy Bridge, Inverness-shire PH25 3DL
kiphideaways.com/hideaways/the-woodland-cottages-cairngorms

ROOMS Five cottages and a lodge sit on the estate, all with stone walls and original wooden beams. Crofton and Kitchen are perfect for families, each with three bedrooms, well-appointed kitchens and living areas where you can spread out and make yourself at home with the stash of books and board games. The cosy twin room in the eaves is perfect for putting drowsy children to bed early, and bathrooms have shower-over-baths, which make bathtime nice and easy. The cottages have indoor and outdoor dining areas, and highchairs can be requested.

FOOD It's all self-catering but there's a small on-site shop that sells pantry essentials and meal kits, all made, gathered or grown as close to the cottages as possible. From winter warmers that can be thrown in the oven to meal kits the kids will love getting involved in and platters with paired wines, there are great options that champion local, independent suppliers. You can even ask for the kitchen to be fully stocked ready for your arrival.

ACTIVITIES It's all about clambering in nature here, whatever the weather. In winter, you can hunker down on the sofa by the log burner in the evenings, and through the warmer months you'll practically live outdoors, cooking on the communal barbecue while the kids go wild on the swing, zip wire and sunken trampoline – and if you follow the festoon lights into the forest, you'll find hammocks between the trees. Bikes for all ages can be requested in advance, and will be waiting for you in the garden when you arrive.

NEARBY The remote location is the real appeal, but there are some great days out to enjoy nearby. Just south of Aviemore, the Highland Wildlife Park is a roaring success with kids and is a haven for Scottish wildcats and other threatened species, and for little adrenaline junkies there's Landmark Forest Adventure Park, a fun-filled theme park with a climbing wall, highwire course, water slides and maze. On rainy days, hop aboard the Strathspey Steam Railway from Broomhill station for a run through the hills to Aviemore and back.

29

GLEN DYE
CABINS & COTTAGES

Outdoor living with creature comforts

Set in the Highlands, at Glen Dye you will feel deep
within the Scottish wilderness without having to sacrifice
the comforts of home. This is the vision of Charlie and
Caroline Gladstone, who renovated what was once a
bunch of dilapidated houses and tumbledown farm
buildings. Glen Dye is now a fun, sustainably minded
retreat for all ages to enjoy outdoor living. There's room
to roam, vegetable gardens, a tiny cinema to discover, and
big starry nights to admire. Festoon lights twinkle in the
pine trees and wood-fired hot tubs and outdoor rainfall
showers allow you to connect with nature as you unwind.
If camping isn't your thing but you want to introduce the
kids to the great outdoors, this is the place to do it.

Bridge of Dye Steading, Strachan, Banchory AB31 6LT
glendyecabinsandcottages.com

ROOMS   The accommodation is eclectic: an American Airstream trailer, a tin-clad bothy, converted farm buildings, a spruced-up caravan, and a coach house that sleeps 12 are among the mix. The decor is bright and homely, with mis-matched vintage furniture, kilim rugs, log burners, and picture windows framing unbroken views. For small families, The Hay Loft and Cottage No.2 are the perfect size, sleeping four, with two bedrooms and a living space filled with books and games. For larger parties, Cuttieshillock (with its lovely garden) and North Lodge (with its river access) both sleep six. Travel cots and highchairs are provided free of charge, and all accommodations have their own wood-fired hot tubs.

FOOD   Each dwelling has its own Big Green Egg charcoal grill and a well-stocked kitchen, and some have Gozney pizza ovens too. An on-site shop sells store-cupboard staples, meat, fish, local cheeses and homemade ready meals, as well as seasonal vegetables from their own garden and fresh eggs from the Glen Dye hens.

ACTIVITIES   From guided foraging to bushcraft (kids will go wild for the fire lighting and axe skills), and more grown-up experiences like whisky tasting and cold-water swimming therapy, there's plenty here to keep everyone busy. There's also a community cinema in a woodshed, a cosy spot for guests and locals to enjoy films with fresh popcorn. On wet days, take cover in The Glen Dye Arms, a BYOB pub with a toasty log fire and record player.

NEARBY   It's blissfully remote here, and that's a huge part of the appeal. There are miles of tracks and forest trails for adventurers of all ages, or go for a family walk up Clachnaben for great views. For an afternoon adventure, the charming fishing village of Stonehaven is perfect for a stroll and some fish and chips. There are also the craggy ruins of Dunnottar Castle and the grand royal residence of Balmoral Castle nearby for topping up on local history.

Caption

30

GLENEAGLES

Luxurious outdoor pursuits in the Scottish Highlands

Fusing five-star luxury with outdoorsy spirit, Gleneagles is a Scottish institution, with as much on offer for wee ones as there is to keep grown-ups happy. While it's renowned for its world-class golf course, there's a whole roster of family-friendly outdoor pursuits, from falconry to pitch and putt, clay pigeon shooting and pony hacks into the Highlands. Then there's the Little Glen crèche for over twos, with a treehouse and slide, toy stables, scaled-down Gleneagle Express railway, and even an off-roading experience in miniature Land Rovers. It's safe to say the kids will be absolutely fine while you slip off for a Dr Barbara Sturm facial in the first-rate spa or take refreshment at the American Bar.

Auchterarder, Perthshire PH3 1NF
gleneagles.com

ROOMS
Rooms marry old school glamour with contemporary luxury, ranging from Country doubles to Royal suites, all with luxuries like pillow menus and fluffy robes as standard and local touches like Scottish textiles. Given the generous size of the rooms, most can accommodate a cot or small bed (some can fit two), and there are also interconnecting rooms. Wooden cots are provided, so you don't need to lug around your own travel cot, and teddies and toys are too.

FOOD
The Garden Cafe and Birnam Brasserie are favourites for families, serving British classics, home-baked cakes and kids' menus. For fine dining, The Strathearn will transport you back to the hotel's glamorous Jazz Age, while Andrew Fairlie's two Michelin-starred restaurant is a premium dining experiences. Little foodies are welcome in all restaurants, though you may prefer to make the most of the hotel's babysitting service. The breakfast buffet is pretty much a full morning activity, and kids will go wild for the DIY milkshake station and pancakes with Wonka-style toppings.

ACTIVITIES
Kids aged two to eight can play, ride Shetland ponies and whizz around a woodland track in a mini Land Rover at the Little Glen crèche. One supervised session is included in your stay, but you can book up to three per day. Through the school holidays, there are daily activities programmes with everything from bug hunting to tennis lessons. You can borrow a Barbour jacket and try your hand at clay pigeon shooting, fishing, falconry and archery; there's also a pool, an equestrian centre, bikes (and baby seats) to hire, a luxury retail arcade with a kids' boutique, and a sumptuous spa.

NEARBY
With 850 acres to explore, Gleneagles has room to roam. If you want to see more of Perthshire's undulating landscape, the team will happily supply maps and a compass, and even organise a picnic lunch. Stirling Castle – the childhood home of Mary, Queen of Scots – is a 20-minute drive, and Stirling itself has impressive architecture and an interesting museum and gallery. Edinburgh is only an hour away, so it's worth the trip to visit the zoo and the castle or scale Arthur's Seat.

31

MIDDLETON LODGE ESTATE

Modern charm and a sustainable mindset

Somewhere to switch down a gear and enjoy uninterrupted family time, Middleton Lodge is a 200-acre Georgian estate, tucked between the Yorkshire Dales and the North York Moors and close to the market town of Richmond. Dating back to 1780, it has been lovingly restored, transforming the old coaching house, dairy and kennels into rooms and residences that feel homely and stylish, perfect for families to relax into a slower pace. Walled gardens are a treat for green-fingered tots, bursting with blooms and crops as they supply much of the produce for the hotel's 'estate-to-plate' dining. For enjoying family walks in the bucolic Yorkshire countryside, watching baby lambs frolic in the spring, and soaking up old-fashioned charm, Middleton Lodge can't be bettered.

Kneeton Lane, Middleton Tyas, Richmond DL10 6NJ
middletonlodge.co.uk

ROOMS There are shepherds' huts scattered among the orchard, cosy boltholes in the Coach House, and rooms tucked into the wisteria-clad walls of the Dairy. With soothing colour palettes and rustic decor, it's easy to feel relaxed. There are dedicated Family Rooms in the Dairy, some with plenty of space for a cot or small bed and others with built-in bunks, covered outdoor terraces and giant jacuzzi baths. The only downside is that normal bath time will never again compare. Cots and small foldaway beds are provided free of charge, as are baby monitors and highchairs.

FOOD The Coach House restaurant champions estate-to-plate dining, with extensive kitchen gardens allowing vegetables and herbs to be grown on-site for use in everything from rosemary cocktails to wild garlic pasta and sorrel gelato. A children's menu offers mini portions of British classics, and breakfast is served from 7:30–11am, with a choice of continental and cooked options. For more sophisticated dining there's Forge, which serves a ten-course tasting menu Thursday to Sunday. The only catch is they have a no-under-12s policy (though babysitters can be arranged).

ACTIVITIES With plenty of green space and the walled gardens, there's ample room to run around. Maps and wellies for the woodland walk can be picked up at reception, bikes can be borrowed for a ride around the estate, and there's a toy box in the residents' lounge filled with classic board games and toys. For something more indulgent, parents can be pampered in the Forest Spa with a treatment in one of the outdoor huts or a dip in the heated outdoor pool.

NEARBY Richmond is a 10-minute drive and worth a visit for its cobbled market square, Norman castle and leafy walks along the old railway line. Mainsgill Farm Shop (which has a great playground and cafe) is somewhere to stock up on local supplies. For an unforgettable unafternoon, explore the nearby Forbidden Corner – a crazy labyrinth of tunnels and follies tucked away on Tupgill Park Estate. With the Yorkshire Dales on the doorstep, walking routes are plentiful – as are proper pubs. Head to Reeth, Gunnerside or Arkengarthdale for walks with stunning views across the hills.

32

NO.1 BY GUESTHOUSE, YORK

City spot where little ones are as well attended as grown-ups

Every inch of this grand 19th-century townhouse feels inviting and perfectly parent-pleasing. Tipis, toys and bedtime stories await in the childrens' rooms, while adults will appreciate the chic interiors, relaxed and personal service, exceptional dining, and the fact that you can explore right from the front door – York Minster is just a short meander. Family-run, it feels sumptuous but is far from fussy. Kids of all ages are welcome, and it's great for younger travellers, who will love playing in the tipis, raiding sweetie jars from the communal pantries and making memories with the Instax cameras the hotel lends for free. At the bottom of a sweeping staircase you'll find Pearly Cow, the bright and airy restaurant, a bar with squashy armchairs, and a butter-yellow lounge where afternoon tea is served. In the basement, the vaults of a former World War II air-raid shelter have been reimagined as spa treatment suites.

1 Clifton, York YO30 6AA
guesthousehotels.co.uk

ROOMS There are 39 rooms and all but the small doubles have space for
cots (which are provided for free). The large doubles have super
king-sized beds, snug sofas and shower-baths, and – if you let them
know you'll have little ones with you – there will be a magical canvas
tipi awaiting your arrival. Nespresso machines are housed within
charming dolls houses and complimentary sweets, soft drinks,
fresh fruit and snacks are available from a pantry on each floor.
If you want to push the boat out, there's a handful of grand suites
with high ceilings, balconies, roll top tubs and extra room for kids
to run around. For those planning a later dinner once the kids are
tucked up, it's worth requesting rooms 1, 2 or 3, which are directly
by the restaurant and within baby monitor range.

FOOD Pearly Cow, the hotel's elegant restaurant, is as much a destination
for locals as it is for guests. Brass tabletops and art-filled walls make
it feel grown up, while highchairs and a Pearly Calves menu ensure
it's just as welcoming for little guests. Out front, a small terrace is a
lovely spot for warm evenings, and the noise and mess that usually
accompanies children's meals is less glaring. Dishes are designed
to be shared, with seasonal ingredients and provenance high on the
agenda. Sample tempura prawns with seaweed mayonnaise, day
boat fish and roast Yorkshire lamb, while smaller foodies can enjoy
fish and chips with crushed peas or sausages with gravy. Breakfast
is a buffet of overnight oats and pastries, with hot dishes and
pancakes made to order.

NEARBY York is a brilliantly manageable town for getting around on foot,
even if you've got a tiny toddler in tow. You can walk along the city
walls, and visit Clifford's Tower, an iconic landmark and the last
remaining part of York Castle, with views out to the North York
Moors. For older kids who enjoy reading *Horrible Histories*, the
JORVIK Viking Centre is a must – complete with the pungent
smells of Viking times. And on rainy days there's plenty to keep
kids of all ages entertained in the interactive Railway Museum.

33

WEST CAWTHORNE BARNS

Rural barns for indoor-outdoor living

Perfect for parents craving a restful few days in the countryside, West Cawthorne is a duo of lovingly restored historic barns in a rural setting on the edge of the North York Moors. Open plan living spaces make it easy to keep an eye on the kids, walled outdoor spaces give you privacy, and far-reaching views over the Vale of Pickering will instantly soothe the soul. The barns are family-owned and created with families in mind. This is somewhere the kids can spend a whole week barefoot. There's no packed agenda here, and no wrestling them out of their PJs to go for breakfast. Instead, it's a beautiful backdrop for enjoying each other's company, playing games, savouring time spent offline, and rambling in the nearby hills.

West Cawthorne Farm, Cawthorne, Pickering YO18 8EH
northyorkshirehideaways.com

ROOMS   The two two-bedroom barns, South Range and West Range, are each set up to sleep four, with spacious bedrooms and ensuites. South Range can, at a push, accommodate six plus two tots in cots, so it works nicely for grandparents or friends to tag along. Calming neutral tones are blended with 19th-century original features, and indoor-outdoor living is enabled with supersized bifold doors that open onto giant patios and private gardens. Once the kids are in bed, sink into your hot tub or just enjoy the downtime, gazing at the view instead of your phone. Highchairs, stair gates and travel cots can be added on request, and each barn has a boot room and utility. There are also two architectural A-frame cabins (equally idyllic, but not quite as child-friendly with their steep mezzanines).

FOOD   These self-catering barns give you the freedom to prepare meals that suit you. Bespoke contemporary kitchens are a joy to cook in, and the open plan arrangement makes it easy to watch the little ones while you're cooking. There's a large indoor dining table for lazy brunches, and a perfect summer set-up outside with a firepit, outdoor dining area and kamado-style grills.

NEARBY   The great outdoors. You'll find mown paths that take you on easy trails through West Cawthorne's farmland, and Dalby Forest is only 20 minutes away and a perfect family day out. There are cycle trails and bike hire, play parks, picnic spots, Go Ape and a Gruffalo trail. For a more adventurous outing, head for the Mallyan Spout waterfall, where a three-mile circular walk will feel like a big adventure for small explorers. You're not far from the coast here either: head for Cayton Bay, a dramatic sandy stretch of the coast, or Sandsend, where you can park right by the beach and share delicious fish and chips at Fish Cottage. Gourmands should seek out Malton, the foodie capital of Yorkshire, full of great delis and pubs and only 20 minutes away. The Talbot Inn draws crowds from far afield.

34

ANOTHER PLACE

An outdoorsy holiday without sacrificing creature comforts

If you like activity-packed holidays in the great outdoors, Another Place needs to be on your radar. On the edge of Ullswater in the shadow of the mountains, this is somewhere you can really enjoy nature without having to forego the comforts of a luxury hotel. You can paddleboard on the lake, hike to nearby waterfalls (you can borrow an off-roading pram for babies and tots), swim and kayak, then feast on wood-fired pizzas, stargaze, and put the children down in their own cosy bedrooms. The hotel feels fully dedicated to family stays (including dogs if you're bringing the pooch!), and there's something to keep all ages entertained both outdoors and in the kids' club. All that said, it is a holiday, so rest and relaxation is on the cards for parents: the indoor pool has a blissful view, plus there's a sauna, outdoor hot tub and treatment rooms.

Ullswater, Watermillock CA11 0LP
another.place

ROOMS Of the 40 bedrooms in the original Georgian house, most can fit a cot or small bed, and there's extra floor space in the Better and Best rooms. If the kids go to bed early, the Family Suites have separate bunk rooms and can sleep up to six. For something a bit different, there are the newly added Outside rooms: a huge luxury treehouse that sleeps five, with two bedrooms, glass walkways and a freestanding outdoor tub, plus six shepherds' huts with log burners, bunk beds, s'mores kits and skylights.

FOOD Families are well catered for with flexible meal times, kids' menus and different spaces to suit the mood. The best spots for relaxed dining are in the Living Space, a casual restaurant with crowd-pleasing menus, and the Glasshouse, which serves wood-fired pizzas by the lake. If you're looking for something more elaborate, a three-course set menu is available in The Rampsbeck from 6–9pm.

ACTIVITIES Kids from as young as five can try kayaking, stand-up paddle-boarding and wild swimming, which all set off from the hotel's jetty and can be arranged as family activities or kids' group sessions. Wetsuits and boots can be borrowed from the Swim Shed. There's also a 20-metre indoor pool where splashing children won't be frowned upon. If you're hoping for some down time, little ones can be dropped off at the brilliant Kid's Zone crèche, which has separate rooms for different ages, and daily supervised sessions are included in your room rates.

NEARBY Hitting the hills is high on the agenda for most people visiting the Lake District, and there are plenty of local routes that smaller kids can manage. Aira Force waterfall is just a few minutes' drive, and there's a scenic 6.8km loop that incorporates Gowbarrow Fell, or a gentle shaded walk to the falls. If it's a nice day, take a boat trip with Ullswater Steamers, or pay Lowther Castle a visit, which has a brilliant garden and adventure playground. For older kids, Treetop Trek is a zipline adventure park 40 minutes away, and for wet days Rheged Centre, three miles away, has a cinema, cafe and great independent shops.

35

KIMPTON
CLOCKTOWER HOTEL

Architectural splendour and city centre attractions

Set in a stunning Grade II-listed building, Kimpton
Clocktower Hotel is an undeniably grand place to stay,
with lofty ceilings, original tiled arches, a glass atrium and
parquet floors, but it's so spacious and bustling that kids fly
under the radar. Day and night, the hotel hums with people
at the bar, in the restaurant and having meetings in the
winter garden – so much so that kids can be boisterous and
no one will bat an eye, and you won't have to worry about
their excited yells echoing around a hushed lobby. There
are plenty of corners and corridors for little ones to
explore, and the spacious Two Double bedrooms are great
for families. The hotel is perfectly positioned for exploring
Manchester's many cultural attractions, and brownie points
for the hotel's midday checkout time.

Oxford Street, Manchester M60 7HA
kimptonclocktowerhotel.com

ROOMS   For those used to more boutique and intimate hotels, some of the rooms here may feel a little corporate – though the payoff is stunning original features, massive windows and roll top baths. No two rooms are the same but overall they're spacious and luxurious, and there are plenty of options for families of all sizes. Those travelling with one child can easily fit a cot or small bed into a standard double room. For older children, the Two Double rooms are a great option, with two double beds in one room – the only catch is having to go to bed when the kids do.

FOOD   Refuge, the hotel's restaurant, spills out of the large dining room and into the winter garden and bar, and has a relaxed, buzzy atmosphere. Kids eat free at the generous breakfast buffet, and while dinner service starts at 5pm, there are crowd-pleasing options available all day – from local specialty pies served with chips and gravy to wholesome salads and flatbreads. The kids' menu will keep tiny tummies happy with smashburgers, cheese toasties, ice cream sundaes, and scaled-down Sunday roasts. There's even a free tuck box for kids on arrival.

NEARBY   Step outside and some of Manchester's best theatres are opposite the hotel, while the Manchester Arena, host to family-friendly shows like Disney on Ice, is a short cab ride. The Science and Industry Museum is a must for inquisitive kids (and curious adults) – interactive, engaging and fun, and only 15 minutes' walk from the hotel. You'll also find dinosaurs and mummies at the Manchester Museum. Manchester is admirably easy to get around with trams and free city buses, and Oxford Road Station is right opposite. MediaCity – the home of CBBC – is 30 minutes by tram, as is Legoland Discovery Centre over at Trafford Park. And for green space, Heaton Park – a half-hour bus ride out of the centre – with its boating lake, playgrounds and treetop adventure courses is a full day out in itself.

36

VICTORIAN HOUSE HOTEL

Cosy and stylish retreat in Beatrix Potter land

The Lake District is wonderful for encouraging little adventurers into the great outdoors, but many of its hotels can feel a little, ahem, stuck in a time warp, with a large proportion angled at older folk who aren't always enamoured with kids running riot around the breakfast buffet. The antidote to this is Victorian House Hotel, which welcomes children with open arms (dogs too) and doesn't feel like a compromise for parents, either. The recently refurbished hotel feels homely but effortlessly chic, with art deco dressers in the parlour, giant vases overflowing with local wildflowers in the conservatory and a stack of maps to borrow for leisurely rambles in the hills. Its pocket-friendly rates seal the deal for us, as does the leafy garden where kids can run free and explore.

Broadgate, Grasmere, Ambleside LA22 9TA
victorianhousehotel.co.uk

ROOMS   With just 20 rooms (four of those in the adjacent cottage) the hotel is bijou. Likewise, the rooms themselves are on the smallish side, but they embrace the quirks of the period building and feel comfortable and uncluttered with their slate floors, upholstered headboards, and colourful cushions and rugs. Most rooms can accommodate a cot but it's worth opting for one of the dedicated Family Rooms, which have more floor space and pull-out sofa beds that are perfect for young kids. There's also a two-room suite in the cottage, which can sleep up to six and offers a bit more freedom if you're putting kids down early.

FOOD   They've done away with rigid lunch and dinner sittings here. Instead, the restaurant serves all-day small plates and sharing boards – a godsend for parents, who have grown too accustomed to a 'bar snacks' dinner of olives at 5pm. Breakfast (which is included in room rates) is a crowd-pleasing affair with bacon rolls, crumpets and the fill-you-up-until-dinner full English.

NEARBY   Located in the idyllic village of Grasmere, this is a solid central base for exploring the whole of the Lake District. Borrow a map from the hotel or ask for them to recommend a local route suitable for tiny walkers. In toddling distance of the front door is Sarah Nelson's Gingerbread Shop, a must-visit for sugar fiends big and small. Legendary in the village and beyond, it's been a site of pilgrimage for sweet-toothed travellers since 1854. The World of Beatrix Potter at Bowness-on-Windermere is only 20 minutes away and brings Peter Rabbit to life through a sensory exhibition, and the small cottage garden is magical and blooming. Brockhole-on-Windermere is another hit with all ages, and has a great playground, cafe, Krazy Karts, mini golf and boats you can hire to go out on the lake.

37

THE TAWNY

Huts, cabins and hideaways on the edge of the Peak District

Like something out of a modern-day Jane Austen novel, The
Tawny lets you frolic in the grounds of the sprawling Consall
Hall Estate, which has been restored to its former glory with
70 acres dotted with lakes, ponds and follies. Dubbed a
'deconstructed hotel', there are 55 huts, treehouses and
boathouses, nestled in woodland or overlooking the lake.
There's an outdoor pool for summery dips and five miles of
pathways within the grounds, so plenty of room to wander.
The kids will love discovering hidden corners, while you'll
appreciate the serene setting, feeling of privacy and giant
spa bathtubs. You're on the edge of the Peak District, so well
placed for taking tiny trekkers into the hills, and the nearby
steam train is always a big hit.

Consall Lane, Stoke-on-Trent ST9 0AG
thetawny.co.uk

ROOMS   While the huts are best suited for two, there are family options among the treehouses and boathouses, which have extra beds and space to sleep up to four. The glass-fronted boathouses are striking, with open-air terraces overlooking the water. The Lookout Family (the most premium of the properties) is a cedar-clad treehouse overlooking the valley, with wall-to-wall windows, a super-king bed, a separate twin room, private deck and spa bath. In contrast to the traditional feel of the grounds, the decor inside is much more modern, with bold colours, velvet sofas and freestanding bathtubs.

FOOD   Two restaurants are housed in the grand main building. There's fine dining at The Plumicorn and a more relaxed set-up at Feathers, which has indoor and outdoor seating and serves sandwiches, salads and light bites. The children's menu is as delicious as the adults', with cod bites, meatballs, pizzas and ice cream. Room service is available, and picnic hampers can be arranged. There's a continental buffet breakfast, with hot dishes made to order (the Staffordshire oatcakes must not be missed).

ACTIVITIES   There's an outdoor heated swimming pool, table tennis, a den-making area for kids to get creative, and bikes (for all ages) to borrow for free. You can pick up a Folly Trail map at reception and explore the grounds, spotting statues, follies and hiding spots as you go. Children's activity packs can also be purchased, including a 'build your own birdhouse' and wildlife bingo. It's worth keeping an eye on their website too, as they host a calendar of ad hoc events, from pottery to painting and stargazing sessions.

NEARBY   The stepping stones at Dovedale will delight little explorers, and there's a nice and easy National Trust route you can follow. The Peak Wildlife Park isn't too far, with its penguins and meerkats, and the Churnet Valley steam railway is a fun day out for all ages. For bigger kids seeking bigger thrills, Alton Towers theme park is a 20-minute drive.

38

CYNEFIN RETREATS

Soul-restoring chalets on the Welsh Borders

Without even trying too hard, this laid-back spot in the
serene surrounds of the Welsh Borders ticks all the boxes
for the perfect family break. Secret play dens? *Check.* Wild
and wonderful green spaces for exploring? Blackout blinds
for easy bedtimes? *Check, check.* Seems they know what
makes kids tick, and parents too, so if you want somewhere
to switch off and relax (yes, even with the kids in tow), this
is it. Comprising three luxury pods and three double-
storey timber eco-cabins, it feels blissfully remote while
being just a 10-minute drive from the bohemian town of
Hay-on-Wye. You'll spend your time leisurely among
nature, enjoying woodland walks and spotting the many
different birds that swoop in and out. Spacious open plan
accommodation makes it easy to relax without having to
chase after children, and you'll have your best night's sleep
ever under thick woollen blankets and dark starry skies.

3 Sheepcote Bungalows, Hereford HR3 5HU
cynefinretreats.com

ROOMS The Luxe-Pods sleep two adults (and a cot or small bed can be provided free of charge), while the Luxe-Lodges have two king-size bedrooms and comfortably sleep four adults plus children, so offer a bit more space for families. Large open plan kitchens allow you to cook while mini-holidaymakers play in a secret den stocked with books and games under the stairs. The interiors are simple but comfortable with huge windows and sliding glass doors, and thoughtful local touches include prints of the Wye Valley, binoculars for birdwatching, books from Hay-on-Wye's vintage bookshops and wonderfully soft Melin Tregwynt blankets. Wooden decking outside means tots can crawl around dirt-free, though there is a boot room with washer and dryer just in case.

FOOD It's all self-catering here, so you've got the freedom to do things on your own time. Kitchens are well-stocked with pots, pans and cooking essentials, and there's an outdoor fire pit (plus marshmallows provided for toasting). Kids are well catered for, with highchairs, plastic bowls and cups as well as Tupperware to borrow for on-the-go snacks.

ACTIVITIES Surrounded by nature, there's plenty of space to roam free. While the pods and lodges have been cleverly angled for privacy, if other families are staying kids will love making friends running around the communal greenery. There's also a garden swing and bird feeders where chaffinches and blue tits gather, and the woodland walk is great for little adventurers, with carved seats and big trees for hiding behind. Once the kids are in bed, it's time for you to relax in the deep hot tub.

NEARBY Hay-on-Wye is just a short drive away, famous for its second-hand bookshops and bustling Thursday market, and there are brilliant views from the castle plus a well-manicured green where we recommend lolling on sunny days. Closer to home, just a 10-minute stroll from Cynefin Retreats, The Bridge Inn is a friendly, relaxed restaurant on the historic toll bridge, serving quality pub grub.

39

THE BARNSDALE

A relaxing family retreat on the shores of Rutland Water

The Midlands might not immediately spring to mind as a top holiday spot, but this honey-coloured former hunting lodge is a destination all on its own, where families can enjoy a relaxing escape and welcome change of pace. Right in the middle of the country, it's a handy stopover on big journeys (minutes off the A1), but equally great for a long weekend, with the beautiful Rutland Water offering a host of family fun. A recent top-to-toe renovation has breathed new life into the hotel, transforming it with tasteful vintage and modern interiors, brasserie-style dining, and a brand new pool and spa in 2024. Family bunk rooms can accommodate the whole brood, and communal spaces feel relaxed enough to hang out in with kids.

The Avenue, Oakham LE15 8AH
barnsdalerutland.com

ROOMS The 45 bedrooms and suites are full of character, with antiques, bold colours, patterned wallpapers and cheery striped fabrics. Even the smallest rooms feel sumptuous, with velvet headboards, plump cushions and luxurious bathrooms. Cots and small beds can be added to most of the Classic Rooms and above, which will work for those with a baby or single child. Dedicated Family Rooms have bunk beds in their own room, and a handful of Rutland Retreats – stylish two- and three-bedroom apartments – offer the flexibility to self-cater while enjoying the hotel comforts.

FOOD Relaxed all-day dining is on offer in the sunny Orangery and 1760 Brasserie, where you'll be served modern British cuisine like crispy chilli squid and grilled lamb rump. The courtyard is a perfect spot for balmy evenings, and you can keep an eye on little ones playing pétanque in the ball pit. Tasty 'Little 1760' children's menus are available, with kid-pleasing chicken goujons and sausages and mash, and a classic continental breakfast spread is included in room rates and will fuel you for the day.

ACTIVITIES There are bikes for all ages to hire for whizzing around the grounds and the edges of Rutland Water, and a welly wall for puddle splashing. You'll find a stack of board games and activity packs for kids in the lounge, perfect for when the weather's not so great, and a new indoor pool along with a spa for knackered parents is opening.

NEARBY Rutland Water is one of England's largest man-made lakes, great for water sports and walking or cycling around, and you can hire bikes and boats or take a Rutland Belle cruise. Given its 22-mile circumference, you're unlikely to walk all the way around, but there are easy paths to cover scenic stretches, a sandy beach at Sykes Lane where you can paddle, and a few playgrounds around the lake's edge. For a change of pace, Aqua Park is an inflatable obstacle course on the lake where you can book hour-long sessions for the whole family – it might be the most fun you've had all year! Rutland Farm Park is a lovely outing for young children, who can meet and feed friendly animals.

40

BARSHAM BARNS

Blissful breaks with cosy barns, beaches and birdwatching

This is a great base for accessing North Norfolk's sandy beaches and scenic countryside. Barsham Barns is a cluster of converted stone barns in a tranquil rural setting, surrounded by farmland, woodland and meadows. Owned and farmed by one family for three generations, the barns have a relaxed rustic aesthetic. Open plan layouts and private outdoor spaces make them feel welcoming for all ages, bucolic views over wildflower meadows and cow-grazed fields will make your shoulders sink, and dogs are welcome too. There are walks from the front door, long sandy beaches you can easily spend all day at, excellent crabbing spts, bijou seaside towns with pubs aplenty and their own microbrewery in stumbling distance.

Green Way, North Barsham, Norfolk NR22 6AP
barshambarns.co.uk

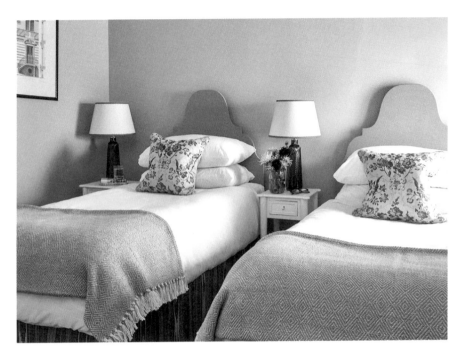

ROOMS   The six barns vary in shape and size, sleeping four to 14. Though
they're fairly close to each other and share a courtyard for parking,
they feel private, so you don't feel on top of your neighbours. They
all have their own outdoor spaces too, either walled gardens or sun
decks, where finches, sparrows and robins bob in, and the kids can
have fun identifying the different species. Inside, stone walls, bold
and colourful textiles, cosy wood burners, spacious living areas
and captivating views make it easy to relax.

FOOD   It's all self-catering here, and the kitchens are well equipped with
pots, pans, utensils and children's plastic tableware. Highchairs
and booster seats are provided for free on request, and some of the
barns have outdoor tables too – perfect for making the most of
warmer days. From April to August, look out for Barsham Brewery's
Street Food Fridays – a must for even the pickiest little eaters.

NEARBY   You'll be 15 minutes from Wells-next-the-Sea, which must be one
of the UK's best beaches for family fun, with its ice cream-coloured
beach huts and long stretch of golden shores for sandcastle building.
Keep an eye out for seals swimming down the estuary, or head to
Pensthorpe nature reserve for birdwatching and eco-friendly play.
The quaint seaside town is worth a wander, with its bustling
independent high street and family-friendly pubs, and the harbour
is a popular crabbing spot, so grab a bucket and join in. There's
ample parking in the town, and you can walk right along the sand
to Holkham too, which is just as idyllic with its dunes and tall pine
tree forest. There's a cafe near the car park, and a great kids'
playground and walled garden to explore at Holkham Hall.

41

RETREAT EAST

A restorative break with cool barns and parental perks

Seek sanctuary in the country with a sustainable stay at
Retreat East, a great base for family days out in Suffolk
with dreamy walks on the doorstep. There are
accommodation options to suit everyone, with cottages,
shepherds' huts and oak-clad barns. Most have kitchens,
which suits families, but you should make a point of eating
in the spectacular Great Barn restaurant, headed up by
Adam Spicer (a former MasterChef the Professionals
winner), who uses produce from the organic kitchen
gardens in dishes that feel refined but not stuffy. Tired
parents can indulge in an hour-long spa session, included
in your stay. You might have to toss a coin to decide who's
looking after the kids, but someone should make the most
of the complimentary 60 minutes in the sauna, steam room
and outdoor hot tub.

Brick Kiln Farm, Sandy Lane, Hemingstone IP6 9QE
retreateast.co.uk

ROOMS   Of the 23 barns, seven are designed to suit families, with two bed-rooms or space for a cot. Decorated in an unfussy style in calming neutrals, comfort is king here, and barns variously feature log burners, roll top baths, wing-back armchairs, and well-appointed kitchens. Burrow, Sett, Cow House and Stables all sleep two adults and two children, with Burrow and Sett having two bedrooms – meaning you don't have to creep around after dark. There's plenty of room in The Piggery and Hayloft for cots (£20, or you're welcome to bring your own).

FOOD   Most barns are self-catering, but dining at The Great Barn, with its vaulted ceiling and open fireplace, will be a highlight of any stay. The atmosphere feels quite grown-up at dinner, with candles and acoustic performances, so you might feel more comfortable dining as a family at lunchtime (the Sunday roasts are particularly stand out). Scaled-down portions and children's menus are available, as are highchairs and kids cutlery. A modest breakfast buffet is included in room rates, or you can order a full Suffolk fry-up or pancakes for an extra charge.

ACTIVITIES   There's ample room in and around the barns for the kids to run amok, before exploring the kitchen gardens and venturing out onto the local footpaths for muddy rambles. A small nature trail with a bug hotel and hedgehog house will delight little conservationists, or there's archery and bike hire for bigger kids. Parents can and should soak up the spa offering.

NEARBY   If the kids don't mind a car journey, hop in and head to the coast. Aldeburgh and Southwold are a 50-minute drive and make for great days out with their blustery beaches and quality fish and chip haunts. Or, you could wander around the village of Orford, stopping to pick up a sweet treat at Pump Street Bakery before taking a short ferry ride over to Orford Ness Nature Reserve (keep your eyes peeled for roaming deer, hare and seals). If you don't fancy getting in the car, it's a 20-minute stroll to the picture-perfect village of Coddenham, where you can have tea at the village shop.

PHOTO CREDITS

Introduction: Glen Dye by Mae Daniels Photography; Barsham Barns ©Barsham Barns / West Barsham Estate; Fforest Farm by Ed Schofield; Harwarden by Mae Daniels Photography; Birch ©Martin Usborne; Harwarden by Department Two. Elmley (first image) ©Holly Farrier, (all others) ©Rebecca Douglas Photography courtesy Elmley Nature Reserve; Birch (first, second and third images) ©Birch, (fourth image) by Steve Wood, ©Birch, (fifth image) by Adam Firman, ©Birch, (sixth and seventh images) ©Martin Usborne; Port Lympne (all images) courtesy Port Lympne Hotel & Reserve; Port Hotel (all images) by Emma Croman, courtesy of Port Hotel; The Retreat at Elcot Park (all images) courtesy of The Retreat at Elcot Park, (first image) by Tom Greenley, (second image) by Alice Tate, (third and fourth images) by Jake Eastham; The Hoxton (second image) ©Tom O'Dell, (all other images) ©The Hoxton; The Grove (all images) courtesy The Grove, (first and second images) ©Helen Cathcart, (all others) by Chris Tubbs; CABU By the Sea (all images) courtesy CABU; Chewton Glenn (all images) courtesy of Chewton Glenn; Three Mile Beach (all images) by Elliot White; Watergate Bay Hotel (all images) courtesy of Watergate Bay, (first image) by Michael Lazenby, (second image) by Holly Donnelly, (third image) by Lewis Harrison-Pinder, (fourth and fifth images) by Megan Hemsworth; The Farm at Avebury (first image) ©The Farm at Avebury, (second image) by Jeremy Flint, (all other images) ©The Farm at Avebury; Mollie's (first image) by Andrew Pattenden, courtesy Mollie's, (second image) ©Elly Deakin, (all other images), courtesy of Mollie's; Calcot & Spa (all images) courtesy Calcot & Spa, (second and seventh image) by Adam Lynk, (all other images) by Jenna Elsby from Studio Collective; St Enodoc (first image), courtesy St Enodoc Hotel, (second image) ©Alice Tate; Lakes by Yoo (all images) courtesy The Lakes by Yoo; The Bull Inn (all images) by Rachel Hoile Photography, courtesy of The Albatross/The Bull Inn; Carbis Bay (first image) courtesy Carbis Bay Hotel & Estate, (second image) ©Alice Tate; The Bradley Hare (all images) by Martin Morrell, courtesy of The Bradley Hare; Artist Residence (all images, except for fourth) by Paul Massey, (fourth image) by Jaz Cottam, all courtesy of Artist Residence; Moonfleet Manor (all images) ©Luxury Family Hotels; Tredethick Farm Cottages (first image) by Joe Lawton ©Tredethick Limited, (second and eighth images) by Sam Oatey ©Tredethick Limited, (third and fifth image) ©Ashlyn Cumberland Reed, (fourth, sixth and seventh images) by Matt Jessop ©Tredethick Limited; Fowey Hall (all images) ©Luxury Family Hotels; Hope Cove House (all images) by James Bedford, courtesy of Hope Cove House; Hawarden Estate (first, fourth eighth image) by Department Two, (second, third and fifth image) by Mae Daniel Photography, (sixth image) by Harwarden Estate, (seventh image) by Markus Brown; Fforest (first image) by Finn Beales, (second image) by Ed Schofield, (third image) by Heather Birnie; Milovaig House (first and third image) ©Milovaig House, (all other images) ©Richard Gaston, courtesy Milovaig House; The Woodland Cottages (first image) by Kirk Watson, (second image) by The Woodland Cottages, (third image) by Rupert Shanks; Glen Dye (all images) by Mae Daniels Photography; Gleneagles (all images) courtesy Gleneagles; Middleton Lodge (first and second images) by Cecelina Tornberg; (all others) by Martin Usborne; No 1 Guesthouse (first four images) ©Guesthouse Hotels, all others ©Martin Usborne; West Cawthorne (all images) by David Critchley, courtesy The West Cawthorne Company Ltd.; Another Place (first, second and third images) ©Jeremy Phillips, (fourth image) by Jim Varney, (fifth images) by Michael Lazenby, (all images), courtesy Another Place; Kimpton Clocktower (all images) by Mel Yates, courtesy of Kimpton Hotels; Victorian House Hotel (all photography) by Jakes Eastham Photography; The Tawny (all images) by Jake Eastham Photography, courtesy The Tawny; Cynefin Retreats (first and third images) by Holly Farrier, (all other images) by Alex Treadway; The Barnsdale (all images) courtesy The Barnsdale; Barsham (all images) ©Barsham Barns / West Barsham Estate; Retreat East (all images) courtesy Retreat East.

ABOUT US

Alice Tate is a travel writer, hotel PR and mum. She lives in south London with her husband and little boy, Kit, and when they're not renovating, they're exploring. Her sense of adventure comes from her childhood, when summer holidays were spent in campervans in Australia or campsites on the Continent, and weekends were spent walking in Yorkshire or the Peak District whatever the weather. These days, she's the one dragging her family out for rain-or-shine adventures. She has a soft spot for Cornwall, fish and chips (with extra vinegar), and the north west where she grew up. @alice_tate

Hoxton Mini Press is a small indie publisher based in east London. We make books with a dedication to good photography, passionate writing and lovely production. When we started the company people told us 'print was dead'. That inspired us. Books are no longer about information but objects in their own right: something to collect and own and inspire.

Want more opinion? Our hardback *Opinionated Guides to Britain* will take you on a tour of the Britain's best bits:

OPINIONATED GUIDES TO BRITAIN

British Boutique Hotels

British Family Escapes

British Cabins & Hideaways

British Family Escapes: An Opinionated Guide
First edition, first printing

Published in 2023 by Hoxton Mini Press, London
Copyright © Hoxton Mini Press 2023. All rights reserved.

Text by Alice Tate
Edited by Gaynor Sermon
Proofreading by Octavia Stocker
Series design by Hoxton Mini Press
Production design by Richard Mason
Cover and map illustration by Charlotte Ager
Production by Sarah-Louise Deazley
Editorial support by Megan Baffoe

*Except for additional images credited on previous spread.

A CIP catalogue record for this book is available from the British Library.
The right of Gina Jackson to be identified as the creator of this Work
has been asserted under the Copyright, Designs and Patents Act 1988.

ISBN: 978-1-914314-51-3

Printed and bound by OZGraf, Poland

Hoxton Mini Press is an environmentally conscious publisher, committed
to offsetting our carbon footprint. This book is 100 per cent carbon
compensated, with offset purchased from Stand For Trees.

For every book you buy from our website, we plant a tree:
www.hoxtonminipress.com

MIX
Paper from
responsible sources
FSC
www.fsc.org
FSC® C163799